BLACK SINGLE MOTHERS AND THE CHILD WELFARE SYSTEM

Black Single Mothers and the Child Welfare System examines the pressures, hardships, and oppression women of color face in the child welfare system and how this affects social workers who investigate childhood abuse and neglect. Author Brandynicole Brooks addresses intersectionality and ideological, institutional, interpersonal, and internalized oppression and how it affects the safety, permanence, and well-being of children. Through research and real-life examples, the reader will be immersed in a historical perspective of oppression faced by Black single mothers involved with social service systems, understand the definition of oppression and its four interrelated facets, examine ways oppression plays out in child welfare supports and services, and discover new integrated methods of addressing oppression. The last chapter discusses theory, generalist social work practice, and transformational leadership styles, which can be used by social workers to advocate on behalf of their clients and inspire self-advocacy, thus transforming child welfare.

Brandynicole Brooks, LICSW, is a clinical social worker who has worked in the child welfare arena for over a decade, providing crisis intervention, crisis counseling, comprehensive family assessment, and focused family counseling. She is also an adjunct professor of social work at the University of the District of Columbia and a graduate of the School of Social Work at the University of Alabama.

BLACK SINGLE MOTHERS AND THE CHILD WELFARE SYSTEM

A Guide for Social Workers on Addressing Oppression

Brandynicole Brooks, LICSW

Routledge
Taylor & Francis Group
NEW YORK AND LONDON

First published 2016
by Routledge
711 Third Avenue, New York, NY 10017

and by Routledge
2 Park Square, Milton Park, Abingdon, Oxon, OX14 4RN

Routledge is an imprint of the Taylor & Francis Group, an informa business

Library of Congress Cataloging-in-Publication Data
A catalog record for this book has been requested.

ISBN: 978-1-138-90301-2 (hbk)
ISBN: 978-1-138-90300-5 (pbk)
ISBN: 978-1-315-69716-1 (ebk)

Typeset in Baskerville
by Apex CoVantage, LLC

This book is dedicated to Mommy, a Black Single Mother, and all of the Black Single Mothers I have ever had the honor and privilege to come in contact with.

CONTENTS

PREFACE

As a social worker in the field of child welfare for the past 11 years, I have encountered many families, all with unique stories. As I moved through my career from the State of Texas, to the State of Alabama, and finally to the District of Columbia, I had the honor and privilege of working with families from all walks of life. Interestingly enough, as a Black single woman with no children, I found it easier to work with non-Black families because our experience and existence were so very different. Through the years I have come to realize that this preference was due to a level of interpersonal and internalized experiences of racism and classism that I was being forced to perpetuate through my position as a child welfare investigative social worker.

Coming to this realization led me to a place of wanting to know why exactly I found myself at this crossroads. I believed myself to be a radical social worker who was not only dedicated to the care and protection of children and youth involved with the welfare system, but I also wanted to help these Black single mothers provide a life for their children without being a statistic. You see, I was raised in a middle-class family headed by a Black single mother who grew up in the Jim Crow South. I never once saw my mother struggle, and I never knew of her experience of racism and sexism until well into my 20s. She, being the protective, ever-mindful mother she was, did not want to taint my vision of the world based on her personal experiences. My mother rose above her experiences. She enlisted in the Air Force after 2 years of college and retired as a master sergeant 20 years later. She was the single mother of two children. Not once did we become a statistic—there was no food stamps, Aid to Families and Dependent Children (AFDC), or even assistance through Women, Infants, and Children (WIC).

Entering into the field of social work was a decision made after initially majoring in psychology, attending one social work class, and then realizing that I wanted to help others not become or stay statistics. In my naiveté, I did not realize my mindset was in line with the oppressive majority. I did not realize that it was not okay to assume my way of life was the best way and I needed to "save" Black single mothers and their children from such despair. My heart was in the right place, but my mind was not. As I matriculated to obtain a master of social work in the heart of the Deep South at the University of Alabama, I was introduced to various other Black women who made the decision to be social workers, but their view on rescuing families from themselves was very different from my own. I learned from my "sister circle" and my professors the various ways in which Black families work.

Part of my shame as a social worker is that I was not introduced to the concepts of Black feminist thought, womanism, and intersectionality until I began to carry a caseload with a majority of households headed by Black single mothers living in abject poverty with intense love for their children, families, and extended kin. My first year working in Washington, DC, opened my eyes to an entirely different frame of thinking to the point that I began to question the practices and policies I once staunchly upheld.

I buried myself in the study of feminist theory and engaged in conversations about the multiple levels of oppression, child welfare policy, and intersectionality. As a result, I set forth to write this book.

It is my hope that through the historical perspective, case anecdotes, and questions for pondering you will be able to see not only the beauty in the lives of Black single mothers, but also what we all as child welfare social workers can do to address oppression.

ACKNOWLEDGMENTS

I wish to personally thank the following people for their support, contributions to my inspiration and knowledge, and for believing in me when I did not believe in myself:

E. Graber, associate editor, Routledge, for making this such a seamless process;

M. Moldvai, past associate editor, for seeking me out at the 2014 National Association of Social Workers Conference in Washington, DC, and meeting with me to discuss my passion;

SJ, for pushing me beyond my comfort zone and helping me to see I had a story to tell;

P. Kratchman and C. Smith, for your consistent hospitality and the use of your writing studio at your little piece of paradise on the Bay;

S. Harris, for keeping me focused, reminding me of my internal greatness, and for being the Zen in the midst of my Khaos;

My Sandersons, for giving me a place of peace when I need to get away; and

To my A-Town Sistas, My Local Bestie, My Other Half, my Fanmi a Chwazi, the Ladies of Kappa Xi Omega Sorority, Inc.—thank you for loving me through this process, for lifting me up, and inspiring me to be great on purpose.

INTRODUCTION

In child welfare practice, social workers and caseworkers come into contact with women with the commonality of the pressures, hardships, and ultimately oppression faced at the whim of the child welfare system. When these women become known to the system, it is expected for them to reach out to their oftentimes nonexistent support systems, learn new techniques of child rearing, and remain compliant for an indeterminate amount of time in order to be reunified with their children. Generally, the support and services provided to these women to address the reason for child welfare involvement have been shortsighted and focused solely on the presenting issues and not on an understanding of the root cause of the struggle faced by these women. Throughout the years, child welfare agencies have moved from a deficit model to one focused on the strengths of the parents and children involved. Unfortunately, the focus continues to be on microlevel changes rather than focusing on the locale of the various types of oppression faced by Black single mothers.

This text seeks to continue discussions of "societal abuse" introduced by David G. Gil (2013) in his book *Confronting Injustice and Oppression*. Here, Gil suggests that "societal abuse tends to affect millions of families through unemployment, discrimination, poverty, malnutrition, homelessness, developmental deficits, ill health, inadequate education, and social deviance as well as through stressful conditions in everyday life" (p. 116). In order to continue this conversation it is necessary to evaluate the history of the child welfare system, the history of women of color involved with the child welfare system, and the broad definition of oppression with a discussion of the concept first introduced by Kimberlé Williams Crenshaw (1989)—intersectionality. According to Graham (1999), "Research evidence suggests that the lack of appropriate preventative support services and a lack of understanding of the cultural orientation of Black families often results in social work operating against the interests of Black children" (p. 104). By focusing on intersectionality in child welfare, this text will provide a historical understanding of the oppression of Black single mothers on the basis of their status as Black, female, and single mother, as well as present ways in which child welfare social workers can advocate on behalf of the Black single mothers on their caseloads and instill principles of self-advocacy.

This text is not empirical in nature, but rather seeks to add to the discourse of best practices in working with families who continue to be overrepresented in child welfare. Throughout the text there will be case examples, with the opportunity for review, assessment, and note taking for greater understanding. Additionally, "Thoughtful Reflections" throughout the text will allow readers to consider their own experiences in response to the impact of oppression in child welfare on the lives of Black single mothers.

References

Crenshaw, K. (1989). "Demarginalizing the Intersection of Race and Sex: A Black Feminist Critique of Antidiscrimination Doctrine, Feminist Theory, and Antiracist Politics," *University of Chicago Legal Forum*, 39–67.

Gil, D. G. (2013). *Confronting injustice and oppression: Concepts and strategies for social workers.* New York, NY: Columbia University Press.

Graham, M. (1999). "The African-centered worldview: Toward a paradigm for social work." *Journal of Black Studies, 30*(1), 103–122.

1

HISTORICAL PERSPECTIVES OF CHILD WELFARE AND INTERSECTIONALITY

Child Welfare Historically

The mission of child welfare across the United States is focused on the safety, permanence, and well-being of the most vulnerable population—children. This mission has been addressed from every angle throughout child welfare's history—protecting children from abuse, educating parents, developing familial support systems, and addressing parents' mental health needs. Currently, child welfare seeks to ensure children's safety from abuse and neglect by implementing permanency planning. Permanency planning is a theoretical social work perspective promoting a permanent living arrangement for children that seeks to meet the child's physical, emotional, and developmental needs (North Carolina Department of Health and Human Services, 2014). Permanency planning means focusing on long-term care arrangements for a child beginning the first day the child enters into the foster care system. These arrangements can involve placing the child with the biological parents, kinship providers, fictive kin, or in adoptive homes. However, prior to the adoption and implementation of this theory, child welfare services turned to practices of infanticide, warehousing, orphanages, and fostering to address the concern of parents' inability to provide appropriate care and support to their children (McGowan, 2005).

According to McGowan (2005), there was no child welfare system in the "early days, however, two groups of children were presumed to require attention from public authorities: orphans and the children of paupers" (p. 11). As a result of this focus, during the 17th and 18th centuries, children were treated like dependent adults and faced one of four different outcomes:

1 *Outdoor relief*: Public assistance programs for the poor provided minimal funds/food.
2 *Farming-out*: Children and dependent adults were auctioned off to provide contracted services in exchange for room and board.
3 *Almshouses*: Institutions were set up by public authorities in rural areas for the care of orphaned children and dependent adults.
4 *Indenture*: Orphans were given to households to learn a trade and were required to continue working for that household until the debt of their apprenticeship was paid (McGowan, 2005, p. 12).

By the 19th century, changes began to be made to address the welfare and poor treatment of children. With the influx of slave importation, the growing size of the bourgeois class, increased immigration, and hazardous labor conditions, there was an eventual rise in the number of orphanages and institutions during the 1830s. These institutions were set up to provide for the care for children whose parents could not provide for them, as well as for true orphans, whose parents were deceased or could not be found. The 1821 Report of the Massachusetts Committee on Pauper Laws found that "outdoor relief was the worst and almshouse care the most economical and best method of relief" (McGowan, 2005, p. 13). In 1824, the Yates Report suggested further support for the increase in almshouses/orphanages in rural areas of the country. However, by 1856 investigations of these almshouses revealed "such a record of filth, nakedness, licentiousness, general bad morals, and disregard of religion and the most common religious observances, as well as of gross neglect of the most ordinary comforts and decencies of life" (New York State Senate, 1857, cited in McGowan, 2005, p. 13) that there was a shift, however gradual, to reforms, beginning with the establishment of the Children's Aid Society in 1853.

The Children's Aid Society was founded by Charles Loring Brace and other social reformers as a way of addressing the poor conditions of the only social services available to orphaned and destitute children. The Society brought the beginnings of a "foster care" system by placing children in "Christian homes in the country, where they would receive solid moral training and learn good work habits" (McGowan, 2005, p. 14). From 1853 to 1929, the Society was responsible for moving more than 150,000 children from New York City to farms across the country to uphold this mission. Also during this time, the Children's Home Society (CHS) was established as a child-placing agency to provide free foster homes for dependent children. However, negative reports regarding child labor, poor hygiene, poor treatment, and abuse plagued the Children's Home Society, and more reforms were seen as necessary.

Towards the latter part of the 19th century, authorities began to "recognize families had an obligation to provide for their children's basic needs" (McGowan, 2005, p. 16) and that if the families did not provide for their children, society then had the obligation to intervene on the children's behalf. Thus, child protection came into play. Child protection was first formally addressed with the establishment of the New York Society for the Prevention of Cruelty to Children (NYSPCC) in 1875. This society was founded following the rescue of Mary Ellen Wilson, which was supported by a leader of what is now known as the American Society for the Prevention of Cruelty to Animals or the ASPCA.

The ASPCA and Child Welfare

A child by the name of Mary Ellen Wilson was born to parents Francis and Thomas Wilson in 1864 in New York City. Shortly after Mary Ellen's birth, her father passed and her mother was left with no source of income. Due to her inability to care for her infant daughter with no income, Francis Wilson sent her daughter to a boarding home with a woman by the name of Mary Score. With the stresses of maintaining her household, and an inability to keep up with boarding payments, Francis stopped visiting her daughter at the boarding home, and Mary Ellen was soon turned over to the city's Department of Charities by Mary Score. At the age of 2, Mary Ellen was then illegally placed by the Department, without proper documentation and little to no oversight, in the home of Mary and Thomas McCormack. Mr. McCormack claimed to be Mary Ellen's biological father. Shortly after this placement, Mary Ellen's second father, Thomas McCormack, passed. Mary McCormack married Francis Connolly, and the new family moved to a tenement known as Hell's Kitchen on West 41st Street in New York.

Mary Ellen was severely abused and neglected at the hands of Mary McCormack Connolly to the point that neighbors became involved and the family moved to another tenement, but not before a missionary, Ms. Etta Angell Wheeler, took notice of Mary Ellen's plight in 1847. Upon seeing the bruised and malnourished 10-year-old Mary Ellen, Ms. Wheeler began to seek ways to legally protect the child. However, there were no local laws that prohibited the excessive discipline of children, and New York City authorities were hesitant to intervene on behalf of the child due to a misinterpretation of the city's early child neglect laws.

Not wanting to leave Mary Ellen in her current state, Ms. Wheeler remained diligent and sought the assistance of Henry Baugh, a leader of the animal humane movement later known as the American Society for the Prevention of Cruelty to Animals (ASPCA). Mr. Baugh's involvement proved to be substantial to getting Mary Ellen's case before legal authorities. Based on Mary Ellen's own testimony and the statements of her neighbors regarding her experience of abuse and neglect, Mary Ellen was placed under the control of the state, and Mary McCormack Connolly was sentenced to 1 year of hard labor. Mary Ellen was then placed in an institutional shelter for adolescent girls.

(Adapted from the American Humane Society, 2013)

Slowly, over the next several decades, the United States would see an increase in the number of societies developed to prevent cruelty to children. However, not until the creation of the federal Children's Bureau in 1912 were there governmental protections for children. The Children's Bureau was not authorized to work at the state and local level until the passing of the New Deal in 1935 under the presidency of Franklin D. Roosevelt. Beginning with the Social Security Act of 1935, the federal government began to focus on child welfare and putting funding and policies in place to address child protection.

Table 1.1 provides a brief overview of some of the more important federal child protection laws.

Table 1.1 **U.S. Child Protection Laws**

Title IV-B of the Social Security Act of 1935	States were provided funding to support both preventative and protective services to children and families identified as vulnerable.
Child Abuse Prevention and Treatment Act of 1974	States were provided funding to prevent, identify, and address child abuse and neglect.
Title XX of the Social Security Act of 1975	States were granted funds to support social services (child protection, prevention, and treatment programs, foster care and adoption services) to low-income families.
Indian Child Welfare Act of 1978	Allowed tribal governments to determine the custody of Native American children and emphasized the significance of placement with extended family.
Adoption Assistance and Child Welfare Act of 1980	Set up mandatory guidelines for states to offer child protection and prevention services to children in their homes, prevent foster care placements, and focus on family reunification; also supported states in paying adoption expenses for children with special needs.

(Continued)

Table 1.1 **(Continued)**

Adoption and Safe Families Act of 1997	Increased funding to states for promoting safe and stable families; required states to move children into permanent homes by terminating parental rights more quickly and pushing for adoption.
Child Abuse Prevention and Enforcement Act of 2000	Established the use of federal funds to enforce child abuse and neglect laws, promote programs designed to prevent child abuse and neglect, and establish or support cooperation between law enforcement and media to support the identification of suspected criminal offenders.
Keeping Children and Families Safe Act of 2003	Emphasized enhanced connections between child protective services agencies and public health, mental health, and developmental disabilities agencies.
Child and Family Services Improvement Act of 2006	Reauthorization of the Keeping Families Safe Act of 2003
Fostering Connections to Success and Increasing Adoptions Act of 2008	Amended the Social Security Act to connect and support relative caregivers, improve outcomes for children in foster care, and provide tribal foster care and adoption services.
Child and Family Services and Improvement and Innovation Act of 2011	Called for improvements in the response of state child welfare agencies to children's healthcare services, length of time in foster care, court involvement, and caseworker visits to children.

As seen in the historical overview and Table 1.1, child protection grew from protecting children from harsh labor conditions to understanding childhood development, which moved the perspective away from treating children as little adults. Today, we see child protection from a child welfare lens focused on ensuring that children's basic physical needs, as well as their psychological, medical, and emotional needs, are met by their parents or guardians. Even with changes in parental expectations, the evolution of child protection laws, and the injection of strengths-based and solution-focused practice within child welfare, today's approaches to prevention and protection still are focused on the shortcomings of the parents as individuals who are unable to meet society's expectations of what it means to raise children. Oftentimes, services and supports ignore the hardships faced by these parents at the hands of a discriminatory society.

The Women's Movement

The women's movement and three waves of feminism are often presented along identical timelines. The first wave of feminism focused on women gaining legal equality with men. The focus of the 19th and 20th centuries was on women gaining the right to vote. The first step in this process began in 1848 with the Declaration of Sentiments, which was loosely based on the Declaration of Independence. In the Declaration, leaders of the women's movement outlined the ways in which "the history of mankind is a history of repeated injuries and usurpations on the part of man toward woman, having in direct object the establishment of an absolute tyranny over her" (Eisenberg & Ruthsdotter, 1998). It then went listed the following to support this statement:

- Married women were legally dead in the eyes of the law.
- Women were not allowed to vote.
- Women had to submit to laws when they had no voice in their formation.
- Married women had no property rights.
- Husbands had legal power over and responsibility for their wives to the extent that they could imprison or beat them with impunity.
- Divorce and child custody laws favored men, giving no rights to women.
- Women had to pay property taxes although they had no representation in the levying of these taxes.

- Most occupations were closed to women and when women did work they were paid only a fraction of what men earned.
- Women were not allowed to enter professions such as medicine or law.
- Women had no means to gain an education since no college or university would accept women students.
- With only a few exceptions, women were not allowed to participate in the affairs of the church.
- Women were robbed of their self-confidence and self-respect, and were made totally dependent on men (Eisenberg & Ruthsdotter, 1998).

Even a brief understanding of women's history finds these outlined complaints as valid. These 12 sentiments were presented and endorsed at the First Women's Rights Convention. In the following years, the woman's movement expanded, and conventions for women were held across the country to increase the voice of the women's movement. The right to vote in 1920 was seen as the first major victory of the women's movement.

The second wave of feminism of the 1960s to the 1980s focused the debate on cultural inequalities, gender expectations, and a new role for women in society. Towards the tail end of this wave of feminism, women of color's voices continued to be silenced or minimized. The focus of the movement was solely on gender-based discrimination, with no mention of race or class discrimination experienced by women of color. The feminist movement began to split, and Black feminist thought began to enter the woman's movement. Black feminists defined themselves as upholding "the belief that women are full human beings capable of participation and leadership in the full range of human activities—intellectual, political, social, sexual, spiritual, and economic" (Hill-Collins, 1996, p. 12).

The third, and current, wave of feminism further expounds upon gender expectations and new roles for women in society. As a continuation of the conversation of the gender and race discrimination of Black women, Alice Walker coined the term "womanist" in her book *In Search of Our Mother's Gardens: Womanist Prose* (Hill-Collins, 1996). In this volume, Walker (1983) provides four definitions of womanist. First, *womanist* was defined as a "black feminist or feminist of color"; Walker then "suggests that Black women's concrete history fosters a womanist worldview accessible primarily and perhaps exclusively to Black women" (Hill-Collins, 1996, p. 10). Further, the phrase "womanist is to feminist as purple to lavender" clearly seems designed to set up this type of comparison—Black women are "womanist" whereas White women remain merely "feminist" (p. 10). Thus, womanism provided the opportunity for Black women to address feminist issues while still keeping the focus on Black communities through the Black Liberation Movement. The term brought together ideologies that at first look might seemed incongruent and gave voice to the experiences of Black women who felt shunned on the basis of race in the women's movement and on the basis of gender in the Black Liberation Movement.

Attention placed on the role of women in society brings to light the expectation of fathers to provide for their children's basic needs, while mothers meet the needs of their children in other realms. Although women have been endowed with this responsibility, they have not been seen as equal to men since the beginning of time. Biological theories and concepts, as well as sociological perspectives, appear to support this continued inequality. Beginning with the earliest stories of Adam and Eve, and still seen today with disparities in women's pay compared to that of men—women have fought and continue to fight to find equal standing in society. In her book, *Patriarchy and Accumulation on a Large Scale,* Maria Mies (1999) presents evidence to suggest that biology has played a key role in presenting females as the weaker of the species due to their physical build and body make up and the expectations placed on them during the Paleolithic era (Richards & Saba, 1990). There is a wealth of research focused on determining the foundation of the sociological perspectives of women's inequality; however, for the purpose of this text, it is not necessary to fully understand the origins of inequality, but rather to understand that it still exists.

From a widely accepted historical perspective, women were not granted equal standing as it relates to political decision making until 1920. Until this time, by law in most states women were seen as property; they were unable to make decisions, purchase property, and at times work in industries other than domestics. During the course of history, women began to find their voice through the women's suffrage movement of the late 1800s and early 1900s. Ultimately, women were pacified with the right to vote; however, it was clear that the voice of Black women was rarely, if ever, heard, as the focus during this movement was on issues relevant to White women. Black women often had to choose between their gender identities and their racial identities. With the reemergence of the modern feminist movement during the 1960s and 1970s, Black feminists became more vocal about the focus of the movement on elevating the "experience of White middle-class women" (Murphy, Hunt, Zajicek, Norris, & Hamilton, 2009, p. 19).

Black women have been seen as less than not only by their White counterparts, but by White and Black men. Due to the history of racism in the nation, Black women are seen as a minority because of their color. Due to America being a patriarchal society, Black women have a history of being seen as property of their Black husbands as well. Therefore, Black women enter the world belonging to two distinct groups who have experienced differential treatment historically.

Black Women

"The symbolism attached to Black women as breeders and sexually promiscuous beings stems from a history of slavery and Jim Crow racism" (Monnat, 2010, p. 642). In their vast works, Black feminists have outlined five specific identities placed upon Black women as a result of this history and the "political economy of domination fostering Black Women's oppression" (p. 642). These identities were not created by Black women, nor did they support the self-interest, self-worth, or self-esteem of Black women.

Mammy: "The myth of the mammy was created as a devaluation and degradation of Black womanhood" (Nance, 1996, p. 546). She was portrayed as demure, obedient, and loving of her White children, even in the midst of having her own. Ultimately, as described by Hill-Collins (1990), the mammy projected "the ideal relationship to elite White male power" (p. 71).

Jezebel: Nance (1996) describes the stereotype of "the sexually aggressive female" (p. 546). This identity placed upon Black women often gave permission for the rape and sexual abuse of Black women: "The stereotype of Black women as sexually promiscuous helped to perpetuate their devaluation as mothers" (Roberts, 1997, p. 950).

Sapphire: Identified by Nance (1996) as "the sharp-tongued evil woman" who "was used to satirize and dehumanize Black women's strength" (p. 546).

Black matriarch: Daniel Patrick Moynihan, the White sociologist and former assistant secretary of labor, placed the blame for the demise of the Black family on domineering Black mothers, or the matriarch. In the 1965 report, *The Negro Family: The Case for National Action*, he argued:

> *the Negro community has been forced into a matriarchal structure which, because it is so out of line with the rest of the American society, seriously retards the progress of the group as a whole, and imposes a crushing burden on the Negro male and, in consequence, on a great many Negro women as well.*
>
> (p. 29)

Welfare queen: According to Roberts (1997), "the contemporary image of the lazy welfare mother who breeds children at the expense of taxpayers in order to increase the amount of her welfare check . . ." which "provides the rationale for society's restrictions on Black female fertility" (p. 951).

Each of these stereotypes "perpetuate the storylines that Black women do not care enough about their children, are responsible for the creation of a fatherless family structure that provides inadequate supervision and socialization of their children, and teaches future generations to be dependent on the government for survival" (Monnat, 2010, p. 646). To continue this discourse further, Thomas (1998) suggests that "efforts to suppress poor women's fertility makes sense only in a context that enables regulatory action" (p. 426). Specifically, she outlines key aspects of a culture of single motherhood. This culture suggests that "poverty is a product of the cultural deficiencies of single mothers" and that "there is a mindset characterized by moral failure" (Thomas, 1998, p. 426). The key features outlined point back to the previous mentioned identities placed on Black women. An additional point made is "poverty is a Black phenomenon and Black women are the transmitters of deficiency-based poverty" (Thomas, 1998, p. 426).

Throughout the history of Black women, we see more often than not Black women raising children as single mothers. In 2012, 67% of Black children were being raised by single Black women, and 66% of those families were living in poverty (Mather, 2010). Single Black mothers have been indicted for the dissolution of the Black community. They have been blamed for the increase of violence within the Black community and are seen as weak from outside the Black community but as strong from within it. Organizations and agencies are in place to support single Black mothers and their children that place little focus on bringing the fathers of their children into the conversation. These mothers are faced with the weight of these allegations, as well as the weight of raising children alone, often in the midst of low employment, limited resources, strained family support, and a myriad of other factors beyond their control. These factors not only add to the stressors faced by these mothers, but they are also touted as key risk factors to be assessed and addressed by the child welfare system. Roberts (2006) notes:

> *The child welfare system not only reflects an inequitable social order; it also helps to maintain it. It assumes a nuclear family norm that gives women the responsibility for caregiving, while denying them adequate government support and vilifying those who do not depend on husbands. . . . Like welfare, the child welfare system is a significant means of public support of poor children, especially poor Black children. The child welfare system also extracts an onerous price; it requires poor mothers to relinquish custody of their children in exchange for state support needed to care for them.*
>
> (p. 46)

It is common practice of the child welfare system in most states to identify the mother as the primary adult or focus client in child abuse or neglect cases. This is tied to the idea of a child's mother always being known, whereas the father may not be a part of the nuclear family. Additionally, child welfare professionals tend to focus on the mother's abilities and inabilities when assessing for maltreatment, because traditionally the mother is responsible for the day-to-day care and protection of her children, as well as providing emotional support and acting as the child's educational advocate, therapist, consultant, and friend. In an effort to address the mother's inabilities, child welfare professionals seek to refer and connect her with services to address her parenting, anger management, financial planning, and mental health, referring her to other agencies to support her voyage towards being a better parent. The shortcomings of this approach, however, are child welfare policies, practices, procedures, and social workers that pay no attention to the interlocking nature of the facets of oppression and the "societal abuse" these Black single mothers face.

Oppression

Oppression is a disease that has permeated all aspects of society since the beginning of time. It is responsible for the construction of the Egyptian empire and the development of North America through the oppression of slaves and the use of force to build these empires. Oppression in North America has occurred since the times of Christopher Columbus, John Smith, George Washington, Abraham Lincoln, Martin Luther King, Jr., and Malcolm X. It still continues today, in 2015, as seen through the lens of the Black Lives Matter movement. *Merriam-Webster* (2011) defines oppression as the "unjust or cruel exercise of authority or power." The *Social Work Dictionary* (Baker, 2003) defines oppression as "the social act of placing severe restrictions on an individual, group or institution . . . the oppressed individual or group is devalued, exploited and deprived of privileges by the individual or group which has more power."

John Bell (2012) of YouthBuild USA defines oppression as a person being "systematically denied equal justice, opportunity, freedom, or the development of their full humanness" (p. 1). He goes on to describe oppression from the lens of understanding its four interrelated parts: ideological, institutional, interpersonal, and internalized. In order for there to be a thorough understanding of the impact of oppression, and to implement ways to address oppression, one should have an understanding of these parts and how they are intertwined. The Four Levels of Oppression (Fig. 1.1) provide a pictorial representation of ideological, institutional, interpersonal, and internalized oppression.

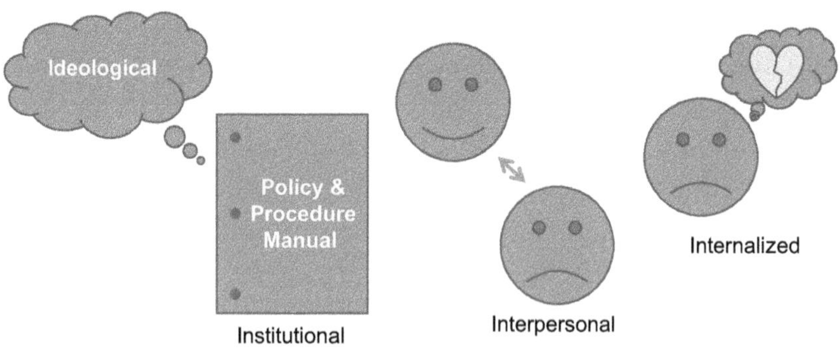

Figure 1.1 **The Four Levels of Oppression**

Ideological oppression is the idea that one group has more power and control or more acceptable characteristics than another. These ideas are held closely by the dominant group about themselves—more intelligence, higher morals, greater work ethic—while the dominant group believes the opposite of the subordinate group.

Institutional oppression then takes that idea and implements policies, practices, and laws to reinforce it. The institution can be defined as government entities, policymakers, and politicians; in child welfare, it can be policies and procedures. Another term used for institutional oppression is structural oppression.

Interpersonal oppression occurs when individuals are, in a sense, given permission by oppressive laws and policies to be oppressive to the subordinate group. Because the idea has been formed around dominant and subordinate, and the law specifically lays out dominant and subordinate, it seems to be acceptable for people of the dominant group to oppress people of subordinate groups.

Internalized oppression occurs when the oppressed, who have experienced oppression through personal as well as professional encounters, begin to believe that they are not as valued, powerful, or acceptable as their oppressors.

"Oppression always begins from outside the oppressed group, but by the time it gets internalized, the external oppression need hardly be felt for the damage to be done" (Bell, 2012, p. 3). For Black women, "there is an interrelated character of race, gender, and class oppression" (Nance, 1996, p. 556). In addition, for mothers involved in the child welfare system there is a cultural understanding and disdain for families with open child abuse and neglect cases.

An Introduction to Intersectionality

In the 1970s, 1980s, and 1990s, feminist theorists, sociologists, and psychologists began to discuss and develop a new perspective of addressing the oppression experienced by Black women. Hill-Collins (1989) notes, "African-American women have been neither passive victims of nor willing accomplices to their own domination. As a result . . . Black women have a self-defined standpoint on their own oppression" (p. 747). And according to Gopaldas (2013), "Black movements led by Black men were sexist . . .

women's movements led by White women were racist" (p. 90). Both of these movements focused either on Black man's equality with White men or women's equality with White men. Neither focused on the interlocking identities of Black women. As a result, as noted by hooks (1981), "no other group in America has had their identity socialized out of existence as have Black women" (p. 7).

To address this erasure of the voice of Black women, the Combahee River Collective, a group of Black lesbian feminists, was deemed one of "the first groups to promote an intersectionality framework" (Mehrotra, 2010, p. 420). This framework sought a complete analysis that highlighted an understanding of the interlocking systems of oppression as it relates to race, sexuality, class, and gender. The Collective argued "we . . . find it difficult to separate race from class from sex oppression because in our lives they are most often experienced simultaneously" (Combahee River Collective, 1995, p. 234).

Kimberlé Crenshaw (1989), who was the first to coin the term *intersectionality*, first discussed this idea in her essay titled "Demarginalizing the Intersection of Race and Sex: A Black Feminist Critique of Antidiscrimination Doctrine, Feminist Theory and Antiracist Politics." She coined the term to describe "the various ways race and gender interact to shape the multiple dimensions of Black women's employment experiences" (as quoted in Gopaldas, 2013, p. 90). Crenshaw's explanation further states "Black women are discriminated against in ways that often do not fit neatly within the legal categories of either 'racism' or 'sexism'—but as a combination of both racism and sexism" (Smith, 2014).

Intersectionality has become a key concept discussed within Black feminist theory and has begun to be used in other social science arenas. The term iterates the experience of Black women as it relates to the various levels of oppression they face. The theory of intersectionality seeks to pinpoint and identify the various intersections Black women face while also introducing the need to address these oppressions in a united front. Addressing only one aspect of an individual's oppressed identity does not move the individual nor the practitioner to the underlying need of facing and defeating oppression. In recent years, the term has moved away from solely focusing on the intersections of oppression for Black women toward identifying similar intersections for everyone. Alexander-Floyd (2012) quotes Crenshaw as saying her "own use of the term 'intersectionality' was just a metaphor" and that she is "amazed at how it gets over-and underused" (p. 4). However, many in the social sciences revere this ideal as an effective tool to combat the oppression experienced by Black women.

Conversations about and implementation of policies, procedures, and case practices incorporating the idea of intersectionality and the various levels of oppression faced by Black single mothers involved with the child welfare system will guide practitioners to a more in-depth understanding of the importance of addressing all facets of a family's identity and will lead to improved outcomes. It is clear there are vast interpretations of and ways to implement the ideal of intersectionality. The intersectional approach has been presented as a technique of both macro- and microanalysis and as having three forms.

Gopaldas (2013) suggests a macrolevel analysis, where the "concept of intersectionality refers to the multiplicity and interactivity of social identity structures such as race, class, and gender" (p. 91). The microlevel analysis then focuses on the fact that individuals live at the intersection of multiple identities, and thus see social advantages as well as disadvantages based on membership in the dominant or subordinate group.

Crenshaw (1991) carries her original conceptualization of intersectionality further by introducing three forms of intersectionality: structural, political, and representational. These three forms can be closely tied to the four levels of oppression discussed earlier. *Structural intersectionality* refers to "ways deeply embedded inequalities not only amplify, but also uniquely define, women of color's confrontations with both sexism and racism" (Alexander-Floyd, 2012, p. 8). *Political intersectionality* is equivalent to the institutional level of oppression in which there is a focus on the plight of Black men and White women as seen through antiracist and feminist laws and practices. *Representational intersectionality* speaks to interpersonal and internalized oppression; specifically, ways in which "cultural representations of Black women condone violence against Black women and the lack of response thereto" (p. 8).

Up to this point, a conversation about the impact of intersectionality in the lives of women involved with the child welfare system has not been breached. A number of texts discuss the concept and impact of intersectionality; however, these texts do not include a specific focus on the child welfare system. This text will not only identify ways in which Black single mothers experience oppression from an intersectional lens, but will also introduce strategies and techniques child welfare social workers can implement to advocate on behalf of their clients to address this oppression and to instill them with a spirit of self-advocacy.

Sarah Catherine is an African American woman who is a recent graduate with a bachelor's degree in political science. She attended a prestigious school in the north and graduated at the top of her class and as only one of three female students. During her final semester of coursework, Sarah Catherine began seeking internships both locally and with various political offices in Washington, DC, and in the southern states of Georgia and Alabama.

Sarah Catherine was called in for an interview at three of the four political offices to which she applied. During the course of her interviews she was asked about her writing skills, typing skills, and ability to file. In conversations with Michael Erikson, a fellow graduate with equivalent experience and GPA, Sarah Catherine discovered that Michael was not asked these same questions.

After attending several interviews, receiving the same questions, and sharing the outcomes with Michael, he suggested to Sarah Catherine that she be grateful for the opportunity to get her foot in the door and work her way up. While Michael was offered a position as a political analyst, Sarah Catherine finally agreed with Michael's sentiment and accepted a position as a clerk.

Although simplistic in nature, this brief scenario illustrates both the concepts of oppression from all four facets as well as the experience of intersectionality at play.

The vocation of humanization is "thwarted by injustice, exploitation, oppression, and the violence of the oppressors; it is affirmed by the yearning of the oppressed for freedom and justice, and by their struggle to recover their lost humanity" (Freire, 1970, p. 44). Women involved in the child welfare system have been dehumanized based on their race, gender, parentage, and involvement with the child welfare system. *Black Single Mothers and the Child Welfare System: A Guide for Social Workers on Addressing Oppression* seeks to return the humanization of these women.

References

Alexander-Floyd, N. (2012). Disappearing acts: Reclaiming intersectionality in the social sciences in a post-Black feminist era. *Feminist Formations, 24*(1), 1–25.

American Humane Society (2013). Mary Ellen Wilson. Retrieved from http://www.americanhumane.org/about-us/who-we-are/history/mary-ellen-wilson.html

Barker, R.L. (2003). *The social work dictionary* (5th ed.). Washington, DC: NASW Press.

Bell, J. (2012). The four "I's" of oppression. YouthBuild USA. Retrieved from https://www.youthbuild.org/sites/youthbuild.org/files/Four%20Is.pdf

Combahee River Collective. (1995). Combahee River Collective statement. In B. Guy-Sheftall (Ed.), *Words of fire: An anthology of African American feminist thought.* New York, NY: New Press.

Crenshaw, K. (1989). Demarginalizing the intersection of race and sex: A black feminist critique of antidiscrimination doctrine, feminist theory, and antiracist politics. *University of Chicago Legal Forum, 140,* 139–167.

Crenshaw, K. (1991). Mapping the margins: Intersectionality, identity politics, and violence against women of colour. *Stanford Law Review, 43,* 1241–1299.

Eisenberg, B., & Ruthsdotter, M. (1998). Living the legacy: The women's rights movement 1848–1998. *National Women's History Project.* Retrieved April 30, 2015, from http://www.nwhp.org/resources/womens-rights-movement/history-of-the-womens-rights-movement/

Freire, P. (1970). *Pedagogy of the oppressed.* New York: Continuum International.

Gopaldas, A. (2013). Intersectionality 101. *Journal of Public Policy & Marketing, 32,* 90–94.

Hill-Collins, P. (1989) The social construction of Black feminist thought. *Signs, 14*(4), 745–773.

Hill-Collins, P. (1990). *Black feminist thought: Knowledge, consciousness, and the politics of empowerment.* New York, NY: Routledge.

Hill-Collins, P. (1996). What's in a name? Womanism, Black feminism, and beyond. *The Black Scholar, 26*(1), 9–17.

hooks, b. (1981). *Ain't I a woman: Black women and feminism.* Boston: South End Press.

Mather, M. (2010). U.S. children in single-mother families. Population Reference Bureau Data Brief. Retrieved from http://www.prb.org/pdf10/single-motherfamilies.pdf

McGowan, B.G. (2005). Historical evolution of child welfare services. In G.P. Mallon and P. McCartt Hess (eds.), *Child welfare in the twenty-first century* (pp. 21–46). New York, NY: Columbia University Press.

Mehrotra, G. (2010). Toward a continuum of intersectionality theorizing for feminist social work scholarship. *Journal of Women and Social Work, 24*(4), 417–430.

Merriam-Webster. (2011). Oppression. Retrieved from http://www.merriam-webster.com/dictionary/oppression

Mies, M. (1999). *Patriarchy and accumulation on a large scale.* New York, NY: Zed Books

Monnat, S. (2010). Toward a critical understanding of gendered color-blind racism within the US welfare institution. *Journal of Black Studies, 40*(4), 637–652.

Murphy, Y., Hunt, V., Zajicek, A., Norris, A., & Hamilton, L. (2009). *Incorporating intersectionality in social work practice, research, policy, and education.* Washington, DC: NASW Press.

Nance, T.A. (1996). Hearing the missing voice. *Journal of Black Studies, 26*(5), 543–559.

North Carolina Department of Health and Human Services. (2014). Definition of permanency planning. Child Placement Services. Retrieved August 22, 2014, from http://info.dhhs.state.nc.us/olm/manuals/dss/csm-10/man/CSs1201c6–02.htm

Richards, S., & Saba, P. (1990). Basis of women's oppression. *Encyclopedia of Anti-Revisionism.* Retrieved https://www.marxists.org/history/erol/uk.hightide/basis.htm

Roberts, D. (1997). Unshackling Black motherhood. *Michigan Law Review, 95*(4), 938–964.

Roberts, D. (2006). "Feminism, Race and Adoption Policy." In *Incite! Women of Color Against Violence* (pp. 45–53) Cambridge, MA: South End Press.

Smith, S. (2014). Black feminism and intersectionality. *International Socialist Review, 91.* Retrieved from http://isreview.org/issue/91/black-feminism-and-intersectionality

Thomas, S. (1998). Race, gender, and welfare reform: The antinatalist response. *Journal of Black Studies, 28*(4), 419–446.

Walker, A. (1983). *In search of our mother's gardens.* New York, NY: Harcourt, Brace Jovanovich.

2

OPPRESSION IN CHILD WELFARE

A Separate Child Welfare System

"The history of child welfare services prior to the passage of the Social Security Act of 1935 is essentially a history of services for White children" (McGowan, 2005, pp. 24–25). Black children who were deemed dependent and who were not sold away from their parents were cared for in almshouses and not allowed placement in private orphanages. Even more contemporary research fails to address the experiences of Black children as it relates to the history of child welfare. In her article "Past, Present, and Future Roles of Child Protective Services," Schene (1998) discusses the history of child welfare from the 1700s to the present with no mention of the oppressive and discriminatory experiences of Black children and families. Due to the biases of the White middle class, there is little information about the social services offered to Black families prior to the inception of Black women's clubs and their response to child welfare (Roberts, 2006).

Prior to the work of the Black women's clubs, child welfare services took the stance of punishing parents by removing their children from their care. This, unfortunately, still tends to be common practice of child welfare agencies across the nation today. Black families have experienced oppression from the child welfare perspective since the beginning of time. The initial response to children who were deemed dependent and destitute was to criminalize them and put them in prison, whereas their White counterparts were placed in private orphanages or taken by train out of the urban cities and placed in rural communities with the opportunity for advancement.

By the early 1900s, Black women's clubs "established a separate child welfare system for their race" (Roberts, 2006, p. 959) focused not only on the welfare and protection of Black children, but also on "resisting racial injustice, advancing the race, and reforming society [by] properly educating and caring for the next generation" (p. 959). The emphasis for these women was on the prevention of child abuse and neglect along with increasing a mother's employable skills by providing laboratories for training women for leadership roles and providing educational opportunities for children. The Black women's clubs opened kindergartens, day cares, and reading rooms and provided for vocational training of the mothers. Over the course of 30 years, the child welfare system set up for Black families by Black women's clubs provided increased educational opportunities for young Black children. In addition, they opened homes for working girls who were oftentimes young parents so that they could continue their education and training and receive protection against being prostituted. This system provided housing, employment, and training in domestic service for thousands of Black women and girls who would have been lost in the punitive child welfare system set up for White children and families. During this time, the membership of Black women's clubs understood that "the well-being of individual Black children was inextricably linked to the status of their entire race" (p. 961).

During the development of a separate child welfare system by the Black women's clubs, in 1910 the National Urban League was founded, with a focus on providing child welfare services to both Black and White families. According to McGowan (2005), "the changes taking place in the child welfare system itself created greater openness to black children" (p. 25). There was an increase in facilities for Black children, and agencies changed their discriminatory practices and allowed for Black foster parents to foster Black children. Ultimately, at the White House Conference on Children in 1930 there was finally consensus that

Black children should be afforded the same care and protection as White children. The difference between the work of the Black women's clubs and the National Urban League was that whereas the former sought to ensure the well-being of and uplift an entire race, the latter sought to punitively criminalize Black parents.

With the political reform and federal oversight of the child welfare system and the introduction of the child welfare provisions in the Social Security Act of 1935, the Black child welfare system was forced into compliance with the expectations of the White majority. These changes led to the public welfare system serving fewer White children and more and more Black children. This, in turn, led to an increase in federal spending on out-of-home care and the beginnings of overrepresentation of Black children in child welfare and more subtle forms of discrimination and oppression of Black children and families. According to Roberts (2006), by the 1970s "policymakers have accepted a medical and individualistic model of child abuse that erases the reasons for poor families' hardships by attributing them to parental deficits and pathologies" (pp. 971–972).

Forms of Racism

The pathologies often identified in Black single mothers are the direct result of various conceptualizations of racism. The key is also understanding that there is a level of sexism that Black single mothers face, thus bringing intersectional theory into play. Before delving into the application of intersectional theory, an exploration of the various forms of racism is needed. In "Toward a Critical Understanding of Gendered Color-Blind Racism Within the U.S. Welfare Institution," Monnat (2010) reviews four forms of racism that build one upon the other to present a case for the experience of oppression by Black single mothers at the hands of the social welfare institution. These four forms of racism are *internal colonialism,* as presented by Blauner (2001); *systemic racism,* expounded upon by Feagin (2001); *color-blind racism,* introduced by Bonilla-Silva (2001); and *gendered racism,* as explained by Monnat (2010) herself.

Blauner (2001) presents internal colonialism as race occupying every aspect of our individual experiences and views racism as being "built into the structure of major institution and maintaining special privileges and power for Whites" (Monnat, 2010, p. 640). Systemic racism then speaks to racial stereotypes that are a part of society's framework of knowledge about racial issues. Color-blind racism, introduced by Bonilla-Silva (2001), details a framework arguing that "societies allocate economic, political, social, and psychological rewards along socially constructed racial lines" (p. 11). This idea is the most important in comprehending the state of racial minorities, particularly women, when it comes to involvement with the welfare or the child welfare system. To carry this further, Monnat (2010) suggests the importance of understanding the impact of racial ideologies as is relates to Black women's experiences with the social welfare system. *Racial ideologies* can be defined as a "racially based framework used by actors to explain and justify the status quo" (Bonilla-Silva, 2003, p. 12). These ideologies serve to provide narratives that support ideological, institutional, and interpersonal oppression, thus making it comfortable for the majority to justify the "perpetuation of a racist social structure by placing responsibility for poverty on Black (women) themselves" (Monnat, 2010, p. 641).

As noted in Chapter 1, Black single mothers throughout history have been devalued as mothers from the position of various stereotypes—the mammy, the Jezebel, the Sapphire, the Black matriarch, and the lazy welfare queen. "Taken together, the seamless web of promiscuity, welfare dependent, single mother families, and race function as a highly effective culture of single motherhood image" (Thomas, 1998, p. 430), an image that suggests that Black single mothers are incapable of caring for their children.

Gendered racism speaks to the connection of the racial ideologies introduced by Bonilla-Silva and the stereotypical identities placed on Black women throughout history. The result of gendered racism is "Black women suffering stigmas that are applied only to them" (Monnat, 2010, p. 642).

Overrepresentation

Here, *overrepresentation* refers to the number of Black children involved in child welfare being disproportionately higher than the number of Black children in the general population. "African-American children are represented among those housed in foster care at more than twice the rate of their overall representation the US population" (Foster, 2012, p. 93). As of 2004, 15% of U.S. children were African American, but 34% of children in foster care were African American (US GAO, 2007). According to Chand (2000), "Black children and families may, due to a number of factors, be more or less likely to be subjected to child abuse investigations" (p. 67). These factors include the pathologizing of Black families and their culture and a cultural relativism perspective that suggests that adaptation and assimilation are the best responses to cultural differences. Other factors identified as racial discrimination against Black single mothers include the overreaction of child welfare agencies to allegations of abuse at the hands of Black single mothers and the disproportionate number of impoverished Black families (Foster, 2012). Chand (2000) further identifies "language difficulties, child-rearing differences, poverty, inadequate legislation, Eurocentric assessment tools, and racist ideology and practice" (p. 67) as factors that contribute to the overrepresentation of Black families in child welfare cases. Still others suggest that mandated reporters—professionals who work regularly with children and are required by law to make reports of suspected abuse or neglect—are reluctant to make reports against White families, and child abuse investigators, once called, are more lenient towards White parents than Black parents (Hill, 2001).

Overrepresentation of Black children in child welfare is also attributed to the idea that there is one way to raise a "normal" or "ordinary" child. Cultural differences in child rearing and disciplinary practices may be seen as deviant, and social workers may tend to lean towards moral judgments based on their own experiences. As stated, Black single mothers raising their children at or below the poverty line are more likely to be involved with the child welfare system. The stressors related to raising children with limited resources place a high level of distress on these single parents, which can lead to more "power-assertive disciplinary encounters" that "are generally less supportive of their children" (McLoyd, 1990, p. 322). This can lead to Black parents being seen as overly strict and domineering, thus, in the minds of social workers, placing children at greater risk for abuse (Chand, 2000). Black families may further be pathologized due to social workers believing that the parents have too many children and the parents have inadequate coping mechanisms. Social workers also often incorrectly assume that Black families have extended family support, and therefore fail to strengthen these supports.

From the child's perspective, increased rates of depression and behavioral and social disorders and lower self-confidence are correlated with an experience of living in poverty, which is linked to higher rates of child abuse (Hill, 2001).

A Mother's Perspective

"Child welfare has for the last century been a 'women's' field. Women have not only dominated the ranks of clients, frontline workers, and support staff, but child welfare itself focuses on the women's world of caring for children" (Swift, 1995, p. 486). Research over the years has shown that families involved with child welfare are typically "poor, many are single, and many are members of racial minorities" (p. 490). Although this research is 20 years old, it still holds true today. Studies within the child welfare arena show Black single mothers being identified as the number one "perpetrators" of abuse and neglect across the nation. According to Lash (2014), "race correlates with involvement in the child welfare system more closely than poverty" and "the system is most aggressive in taking action against Black single mothers." This change in the color of the child welfare system, coupled with the various forms of racism and levels of oppression, place Black single mothers in a precarious position when it comes to reunifying with their children. Literature representative of child welfare for the past two decades has placed the blame on single mothers for the poor quality of care for their children.

Considering a trauma-focused lens, which provides an understanding of the underlying issues that these mothers may face, the *Journal of Child Abuse and Neglect* (1993) once suggested through studies that abuse and neglect often occur as the result of the mother's childhood experience of abuse (Swift, 1995; Weston & Collaton, 1993). However, it becomes a slippery slope to place the moniker of "victim" on these mothers, because this could lead to further portrayal of these women as "damaged, powerless, and in need of ongoing intervention by child welfare and other authorities" (Swift, 1995, p. 493).

What can be seen in child welfare practices is an expectation for undereducated, un- or underemployed women to miraculously be able to push aside the ideological oppression and structural racism they face in the midst of child welfare involvement. What is well known about families involved with the child welfare system is that in most cases when child abuse and neglect occur the family finds itself in the midst of crisis. Nearly 45% of Black single mothers are unemployed with more than one child living at home, and as the head of the household these mothers are less likely to be employed and more likely to be receiving welfare than their White counterparts (Neville & Hamer, 2001). Often these mothers find themselves living paycheck to paycheck and in the midst of a juggling act. When bills are due, these women must decide between putting food on the table, securing running water, or maintaining electricity, along with paying educational fees, and, depending on where they live, paying for transportation to and from their one, two, or three places of employment. The crisis occurs when a child becomes sick or a vehicle breaks down, or as a Black mother she has all but ignored the debilitating symptoms of depression. When one of the many balls she is juggling drops, this is when mandated reporters, family members, or neighbors contact the child welfare system to make a report abuse and neglect rather than provide tangible support.

These reports are in the form of full-on investigations that seek to identify the mother's deficits, demonize her for attempting to handle everything on her own, and question her about the whereabouts of a man who has not been in her or her children's lives since those children were born.

Once this investigation takes place, the mother is asked to complete a series of services, based on how severe the abuse or neglect has turned out to be. She is asked to attend numerous assessments, evaluations, drug screenings, visitation appointments, doctors' appointments, and school appointments, all while maintaining her two or three jobs and ensuring her children will have a place to come home to once reunification is reached at some time in the future. Due to changes in the welfare system seen with the Personal Responsibility and Work Opportunity Reconciliation Act of 1996, she is now facing sanctions to her Temporary Aid to Needy Families support because she is missing required appointments, job training classes, and educational programs due to requirements placed on her by the child welfare system. In the midst of this, she is told she has 12 months to get herself together or her children will be placed for adoption. Every 6 months she is required to stand before a judge in a court of law, the one place she has dedicated her life to keeping her children out of. She must become a better parent, even while her children are away from her. She must learn to get along with the woman her children are now calling "mommy." Part of her involvement with the child welfare system is to now have professionals in and out of her life on a regular basis. Professionals who are asking her to share her darkest secrets, her childhood traumatic experiences, her failed relationship with her children's father, and the strained relationship with her family. She is being asked for contact information to the mother, sister, aunt, or friend she has not had contact with in several years because of a disagreement about her marriage, her sexuality, or the way she is raising her children.

The above narrative may seem exaggerated or it may seem to oversimplify the experience of Black single mothers involved with the child welfare system; however, it is a combination of the experiences of mothers across the country who are faced with being assessed based on Eurocentric expectations and attending evidence-based programs whose reliability testing was done with families that did not look like hers. All with the expectation that she check boxes, learn new skills, and attend to her children's psychological and emotional needs, as well as her own, while maintaining a sense of accomplishment and esteem in the midst of a broken, racist, and often sexist system.

Deeper still, these single mothers tend to experience repetition of investigations and assessments with the child welfare system even in the midst of their completion of services and supports identified to be in the best interest of the child to ensure their safety. What then is being missed in implementing services for these single mothers? What aspect of the family's life is being misdiagnosed and erroneously assessed?

Child Protection Services

As seen in earlier discussions of the child welfare system, the system evolved from providing food, clothing, and shelter to dependent and orphaned children in hazardous, and sometimes abusive, living situations to one focused on ensuring that parents upheld their obligation to care for their own children. The role of child protective services now focuses on screening families for suspected abuse or neglect; assessing families' abilities to ensure the safety and well-being of their children; and, when families are unable to do so, completing referrals to various entities to assist the parent in getting to a place of being able to carry out their parental expectations.

The investigation of child abuse and neglect seeks to identify the person or persons responsible for the abuse or neglect of a child. There is little focus on a strengths-based, solution-focused model at the time of the investigation, rather, child protective services investigators commonly work from what is known as the *deficit approach*.

The deficit approach was once used in child welfare practice as a means of identifying the parents' shortcomings. The research presented shows that deficits in homes headed by Black single mothers were easily identified based on a history of racism and sexism. This approach often led to a tainted perspective of the mother's ability to follow through with the expectations of her child welfare social worker. Through the deficit model, it became easy to readily identify services for a mother whose children were in care. If the case was opened for physical abuse, it became an almost automatic referral for anger management. If the mother's case was opened for neglect, she was enrolled in financial management classes. If a case was opened due to educational neglect, physical abuse, or other forms of neglect, a referral to parenting classes was made. Each of the referrals did not take into consideration the underlying issues the mother may face. It did not consider her own history or experience of abuse or neglect, it did not take into account that she was simply parenting the way she was parented, nor did these referrals assess the types of services that were being provided. Oftentimes the mother of a teenage daughter would find herself enrolled in parenting classes to educate her on how to effectively calm and soothe a toddler. However, she would attend these classes to be in compliance with her family's case plan towards reunification. She may not have learned a new skill, but she was able to check off a box.

In several jurisdictions across the United States, a differential response is used to address child protection. Depending on where one is practicing, the explanation of differential response can present differently. Differential response is the act of the child welfare agency having individualized responses to various forms of abuse and neglect. In most cases, situations where abuse has been identified lead automatically to an investigation to determine the perpetrator of the abuse. In cases where there is neglect that rises to the attention of the child welfare agency, an assessment of the family's strengths, informal and formal supports, as well as readiness for change is completed. The key difference in these two responses are rooted in the shift of child welfare agencies to practice from a deficit model to a strengths-based, solution-focused one.

As late as 2008, child welfare programs began to shift from this deficit approach to one focused on a strength-based, solution-focused approach. This approach introduced not only supporting a mother to identify her strengths but introduced the use of an individualized approach that called for "interagency collaboration, cultural and linguistic competence, child, youth, and family involvement; community-based services; and accountability" (National Technical Assistance and Evaluation Center for Systems of Care, 2008, p. 1). However, even with the advent of this new individualized focus on family strengths, Black single mothers find themselves with child welfare social workers who are unable to assist them in identifying their strengths because of the intense levels of oppression experienced. It becomes necessary to couple the deficit approach in identifying the shortcomings of the child welfare system while upholding the tenets of the strengths-based model to lift Black single mothers out of the system.

Once an investigation or assessment has been completed with the family, specific research-based assessments are completed to determine the likelihood for future maltreatment, whether it be abuse or neglect. If, based on the child welfare social worker's assessment, the family is deemed to be at moderate to high risk for future maltreatment, then the family may be referred to in-home family support services. These services are supports that are put into place while the children are still residing in the home. Services range from referral to community-based organizations to homemaker services. Often, the family is required to meet at least twice per month with an in-home social worker, whose position is to continually assess the family and determine if the risk has been reduced or ameliorated.

However, if there is an incidence in which the safety threat to the child cannot be controlled through an in-home support case, an out-of-home placement is necessary. Children are removed from the care and supervision of their parents through a court order and placed in foster homes. During this placement, an out-of-home child welfare social worker is responsible for ensuring that the child is receiving medical care, educational support, and support to their emotional and psychological well-being. In some jurisdictions, this same social worker is also responsible for supporting the parents to address any barriers to parenting that have been assessed through the investigation or assessment process. In other jurisdictions, the parents receive a separate social worker to address their needs.

At the time the parent or parents complete recommended services and are able to demonstrate enhanced parenting, coping, and family management skills, the in-home social worker can determine case closure, while an out-of-home social worker will present the family's case to the court and recommend reunification. If parents are not able to work with the child welfare agency to reduce risks or address safety threats, the social worker can also recommend termination of parental rights, thus leaving the child legally free for adoption.

Reentry

Once Black single mothers have successfully checked off all of the boxes and have had little support in utilizing their strengths in a new way, there is the phenomena of reentry with which to contend. When a mother has reached the point of reunification with her child, it is with the expectation that the safety risks have been diminished and any threats to the child's safety or well-being have been ameliorated. This decision is often based on the assessment of the child welfare social worker. Child welfare agencies have limited timeframes to reach a point of reunification with a mother and her children. The Adoption and Safe Families Act (ASFA) of 1997 "reduced the amount of time parents have to reunify with their children from 18 to 12 months" (Wells & Correia, 2012, p. 181). This placed Black single mothers faced with low rates of employment, strict time constraints on the receipt of public assistance, and stringent guidelines from the child welfare agency and the neglect system at a disadvantage. The Black single mother is now expected to overcome decades of oppression at every level in a matter of 12 months, while her assigned social worker, who may or may not understand her plight, must assess her readiness to be reunified with her children. These women are being asked to make the impossible possible.

Research of reentry into child protective services suggests that there are predictors of reentry into out-of-home care from the child, parent, and case perspectives. Based on research conducted by Wells and Correia (2012), "race and ethnicity are strong predictors of reentry" (p. 183). Specifically, Black children and youth had the highest reentry rates. Second, poverty was an indicator of reentry in care, as children whose families received TANF returned to care at a higher rate than their counterparts. In regards to parental characteristics, there was a correlation between parents' substance abuse and reentry rates along with what Festinger (1994) identified as low parenting skills and lack of social support. Finally, studies reviewed case characteristics, and there was a correlation between a child's length of time in care, reason for placement, type of placement (family or traditional), and multiple child protective services investigations and reentry. Separate research findings also suggest that the risk or recurrent maltreatment is greater for children living in single-parent homes (Connell, Vanderploeg, Katz, Caron, Saunders, et al., 2009).

However, hope is not lost. Just as the Black women's clubs of the 1900s sought to address child welfare from a perspective that made sense to the Black single mother, so does this text. As outlined by Black women's clubs, child welfare should resist racial injustice, advance all races, reform society through proper education of children and parents, and care for the next generation through preventive social work practice that addresses mothers' skills and children's opportunities (Roberts, 2006).

In an effort to bring the experiences of Black single mothers' involvement with the child welfare agency to life, the following is a case example of a family involved with the system. The challenge here is to identify ways in which the various levels of oppression come into play and how intersectional theory can be implemented to address the needs of this mother and her family.

In the following chapters, this example will be used to highlight key aspects of both.

Thoughtful Reflections

The Singleton–Betts–Davidson Family

Adrianna Singleton is an African American, 40-year-old single mother of four children: Sarah, age 15; Syncere, age 12; Jeffrey, age 5; and David, age 1. Jeremy Betts is the father of Sarah and Syncere. Michael Davidson is the father of Jeffrey and David. Ms. Singleton is currently unemployed and receives financial support through the Temporary Assistance for Needy Families program. She has filed for child support from both Mr. Betts and Mr. Davidson; however, she has not received financial assistance from either in the past 4 years.

Ms. Singleton was previously employed as a certified nursing assistant (CNA) working at a local senior citizen long-term care facility; however, due to her missing several days of work in a row she was terminated from this position and has been out of work for the past 3 months. Sarah and Syncere were recently considered truant from school, and Syncere was recently arrested for a physical altercation with a 13-year-old at the community bus stop. Ms. Singleton missed work because she had to attend parent–teacher meetings at the school for her eldest daughters, and she had to attend court hearings for Syncere's new juvenile delinquency case.

Sarah, Syncere, and Jeffrey are currently enrolled in school while David attends day care daily. Sarah was born prematurely and thus experienced developmental delays that currently manifest in acting out behaviors. Due to her behavior, an educational assessment was completed with Sarah when she was 10 years old, and she began to receive specialized school support services through an Individualized Education Plan (IEP).

For the past 3 months, Ms. Singleton has been seeking employment to no avail. She feels her previous supervisor continues to downplay her skills and abilities when potential employers seek a reference. During her time working at the senior citizen center, she overheard the hiring manager speak disparagingly about the area of town where she and several of her coworkers lived. This manager discussed his disdain from hiring CNAs from this part of town as he felt the women there were lazy, undereducated, and only worked to ensure their "stamps didn't get cut off." Although she wanted to leave this position after overhearing this conversation, Ms. Singleton knew she would be ineligible for unemployment benefits if she left on her own. Even with this thought in mind, when Ms. Singleton went to apply for these benefits, she was denied on the basis that her employer reported the loss of her job was due to her inability to complete the tasks of her job.

The family was recently evicted from their three-bedroom apartment due to nonpayment of rent, as Ms. Singleton made the decision to pay her electric and water bills and she purchased new shoes for her boys. Currently, the family is residing with Ms. Singleton's stepmother, Ms. Marie Stone, in her four-bedroom home. Ms. Singleton and Ms. Stone do not necessarily get along; however, Ms. Stone refuses to allow her late husband's grandchildren to live in a homeless shelter. Ms. Singleton asked her biological mother for assistance; however, due to continual conflict between them, she did not feel it was in the best interest of her children to reside with her mother.

Ms. Singleton has been diligent in ensuring that Jeffrey gets to his school every morning on time and that David attends day care. However, last week when she took David to his day care center, Ms. Singleton was informed David could not return until she paid the $400 past due amount for day care services. Previously, Ms. Singleton was receiving a day care voucher that covered the total cost of day care services; however, because she was not working or enrolled in an educational program for at least 20 hours per week, her day care voucher renewal application was denied. Following her appointment with the day care provider, Ms. Singleton met with her TANF case manager and was informed that also due to her not working or being enrolled in an educational program for at least 20 hours per week her TANF benefits would be reduced by 50% until she came into compliance with the regulations set forth.

Today, Ms. Singleton received a visit from a social worker with the state's child protective services (CPS) agency. According to the social worker, whom the family has worked with before, two separate reports were made to the agency regarding Jeffrey attending school often hungry and unkempt and Sarah not attending school at all, despite the school's efforts to address their concerns with Ms. Singleton. During the course of the investigation it was determined that there was sufficient information to substantiate allegations of neglect and educational neglect for both Jeffrey and Sarah.

Based on the case example and information presented thus far, consider the following questions. Jot down your thoughts here, as these questions will be addressed in subsequent chapters.

1 What are key areas to address with Ms. Singleton and her family?

____

____

____

____

2 How have the various levels of oppression played out within Ms. Singleton case?

____

____

____

____

3 In what ways can the social worker advocate on behalf of Ms. Singleton?

____

____

4 In what ways can the social worker begin to support Ms. Singleton in self-advocacy?

Addressing Oppression in Child Welfare

In order to address the myriad forms of oppression faced by Black single mothers, child welfare social workers must be open to facing oppression, both racial and gendered, at each level of oppression: ideological, institutional, interpersonal, and internalized. We have the responsibility of guiding the children and families we work with to a position of seeing their inherent strengths for themselves. This means that it is necessary to be purposeful in our use of an individualized strengths-based approach to not only address the allegations that brought the family to our attention, but in identifying the underlying issues. These underlying factors will undoubtedly guide us to a place of having to address the ideas that brought about the policies that were embedded in the practice that lead to the breakdown of the esteem and worth of individuals.

More specifically, working with Black single mothers has to be from an understanding of all other interrelated subordinate identities. We must work in such a way to assist her in overcoming the stereotype of her being a welfare queen whose sole purpose is to have taxpayers care for her and her children. We must seek policy changes that lump all welfare recipients together with the same expectations when there is an evident historical disadvantage placed on these women.

By upholding the mission and vision of the social work profession, we will be able to better serve Black single mothers and decrease incidents of oppression, overrepresentation, and reentry for children into foster care.

The National Association of Social Workers (NASW) is the professional association that sets forth guidelines and outlines a code of ethics specific to the field of social work. Although many child welfare jurisdictions do not require a degree in social work to work in the field, several others do require a social work degree and license. Therefore, the NASW holds relevance to any conversation related to child welfare. The National Association of Social Workers (2008) Code of Ethics states "the primary mission of the social work profession is to enhance human well-being and help meet the basic human needs of all people, with particular attention to the needs and empowerment of people who are vulnerable, oppressed, and living in poverty" (p. 1). Additionally, this code lays out specific core values that guide social work practice. These values are service, social justice, dignity and worth of the person, importance of human relationships, integrity, and competence. Specific to the core value of social justice, the NASW (2008) Code of Ethics states:

> *Social workers pursue social change, particularly with and on behalf of vulnerable and oppressed individuals and groups of people. Social workers' social change efforts are focused primarily on issues of poverty, unemployment, discrimination, and other forms of social injustice. These activities seek to promote sensitivity to and knowledge about oppression and cultural and ethnic diversity. Social workers strive to ensure access to needed information, services, and resources; equality of opportunity; and meaningful participation in decision making for all people.*
>
> (p. 3)

To this point, it is clear that history has placed a level of vulnerability and oppression on Black single mothers. Thus, child welfare social workers have an obligation to implement social change efforts to alleviate this vulnerability and oppression.

References

Blauner, R. (2001). *Still the big news: Racial oppression in America.* Philadelphia, PA: Temple University Press.

Bonilla-Silva, E. (2001). *White supremacy and racism in the post-civil rights era.* Boulder, CO: Lynne Rienner.

Bonila-Silva, E. (2003). *Racism without racists: Color-blind racism and the persistence of racial inequality in the United States.* Lanham, MD: Rowman & Littlefield

Chand, A. (2000). The over-representation of black children in the child protection system: Possible causes, consequences and solutions. *Child and Family Social Work, 5*, 67–77.

Connell, C. M, Vanderploeg, J., Katz, K., Caron, C., Saunders, L., & Tebes, J. (2009). Maltreatment following reunification: Predictors of subsequent child protective services contact after children return home. *Child Abuse/Neglect, 33*(4), 1–20.

Feagin, J. R. (2001). Racist America: Roots, current realities, and future reparations. New York, NY: Routledge.

Festinger, T. (1994). *Returning to care: Discharge and reentry to foster care.* Washington, DC: Child Welfare League of America.

Foster, C.H. (2012). Race and child welfare policy: State-level variations in disproportionality. *Race and Social Problems, 4*, 93–101.

Hill, S.A. (2001). Class, race, and gender dimensions of child rearing in African American families. *Journal of Black Studies, 31*(4), 494–508.

Lash, D. (2014). Race and class in the US foster care system. *International Socialist Review, 91.*

McGowan, B.G. (2005). Historical evolution of child welfare services. In G.P. Mallon (Ed.), *Child welfare in the twenty-first century* (pp. 21–46). New York, NY: Columbia University Press.

McLoyd, V. (1990). The impact of economic hardship on Black families and children: Psychological distress, parenting, and socioemotional development. *Child Development, 61*, 311–346.

Monnat, S. (2010). Toward a critical understanding of gendered color-blind racism within the US welfare institution. *Journal of Black Studies, 40*(4), 637–652.

Moynihan, D.P. (1965). *The Negro family: The case for national action.* Washington, DC: Office of Policy Planning and Research, US Department of Labor.

National Association of Social Workers. (2008). *Code of ethics.* Washington, DC: NASW.

National Technical Assistance and Evaluation Center for Systems of Care. (2008). "An individualized strengths-based approach in public child welfare driven systems of care." Child Welfare Information Gateway Factsheet, pp. 1–8.

Neville, H., & Hamer, J. (2001). We make freedom: An exploration of revolutionary Black feminism. *Journal of Black Studies, 31*(4), 437–461.

Roberts, D. (2006). Feminism, Race and Adoption Policy. In *Incite! Women of color against violence* (pp. 45–53). Cambridge, MA: South End Press.
Schene, P. (1998). Past, present, and future roles of child protective services. *The Future of Children*, Spring, 23–38.
Swift, K. (1995). Missing persons: Women in child welfare. *Child Welfare, 74*(3), 486–502.
Thomas, S. (1998). Race, gender, and welfare reform: The antinatalist response. *Journal of Black Studies, 28*(4), 419–446.
U.S. Government Accountability Office. (2007, July). African American children in foster care: Additional HHS assistance needed to help states reduce the proportion in care. Report to the Chairman, Committee on Ways and Means, House of Representatives. (GAO-07–816). Washington, DC: U.S. Government Printing Office.
Wells, M., & Correia, M. (2012). Reentry into out-of-home care: Implications of child welfare workers' assessments of risk and safety. *Social Work Research, 36*(3), 181–195.
Weston, J., & Collaton, M. (1993). A legacy of violence in nonorganic failure to thrive. *Child Abuse and Neglect, 17*, 709–714.

3

THE FOUR LAYERS OF OPPRESSION AND CHILD WELFARE PRACTICE

Oppression can be understood as prejudice plus power: It is an interlocking system that involves the domination and control of social ideology, institutions, and resources, resulting in a condition of privilege for one group relative to the disenfranchisement of another.
(Gamst, Der-Karabetian, Dane, 2008, p. 506)

Oppression = Prejudice + Power

Members of both dominant and subordinate groups can experience prejudice, or a preference for desired traits; however, because of the implied power of the dominant group through historic ideas and cultural understandings, it can use prejudice to oppress others. "The oppressed person is always dealing with the probable. He cannot succeed or fail—he can only survive. And mere survival, however glorified or imbued with spiritual meaning, is the essence of futility, the mark of an unlived life" (Goldenberg, 1978, p. 4).

As previously discussed, oppression has four layers.

Ideological Oppression

Ideological oppression is likely the most difficult level of oppression to delineate and fully research, because it is a level of oppression whose origins are rooted in the thoughts of one group being subordinate to another based on the social constructs of race, gender, and class. It is difficult to assess the foundations of the thoughts of individuals, which then become the thoughts of a collective.

The idea of one group of people being better than another group has permeated the history of America since its discovery. This idea has shaped the ways in which people have been either granted advantages or in which disadvantages have fallen upon an entire class of people. A cursory view of American history will lead anyone to see the subordinate and dominant separation of White and Black people and men and women. Although activists and movements have sought to combat ideological oppression, remnants of it remain. Neville and Hamer (2001) explain that "ideology can be defined as a system within its own logic and rigor of representations endowed with a historical existence and a role within a given society" (p. 449). Recall the earlier discussion of racial ideology as a means to protect the status quo of people of color, namely those of African descent being the subordinate group. Neville and Hamer (2001) suggest that this status quo can also be expanded to cover gender identity: "Gender ideologies are manifested and perpetuated by false representations of women as inferior" (p. 449). This is seen in the characterization of women as the weaker, emotional, and skillfully challenged sex. For Black women, the separation of the subordinate and dominant group has left them far outside the margins of respectability and humanization. Black women's experience of oppression on an ideological level comes from the interlocking of their identities as Black and also as women.

As expressed by Hill (2001), the family was socially constructed to be a two-parent household with a father who worked to support his family and a mother who stayed at home with the children. This ideal began during the time of industrialization. However, this was never the makeup of the Black family, but was forced as a result of ownership, and thus assimilation to the expectations and ideals of the slave owner.

For centuries, Black women have been seen as the mammies of a generation of White children, forced to raise, nurture, and love White children, with their own being sold away from them into slavery. Also as a result of this time, Black women were being used as sexual objects for slave owners, and thus over time became seen as hypersexualized beings unfit for motherhood.

Those Black women who maintained a connection to the African culture of being the matriarch in their families were looked down upon for not adapting or assimilating in a way that "supports the collective interests of the dominant culture" (Graham, 1999, p. 106). Moving from the place of slavery towards the civil rights movement, the Black women's voice was often left out of the movement due to the sexist attitudes and ideals of the Black men focused so heartily on gaining equality with White men.

Within the child welfare and social welfare system, ideological oppression is seen with one "Nurse Brown" whose belief is "most Black women should have their tubes tied and that birth control should be put in the drinking water in Black communities" (Roberts, 1997, p. 947). This may be a direct quote from one nurse nearly 20 years ago, but the idea still floods policies, practices, and procedures within these systems today. These ideologies directly affect Black single mothers, as these created ideologies justify and often normalize certain racial phenomena within the social welfare system, specifically higher rates of social welfare use and sanctioning among Black families (Monnat, 2010).

Along with these ideas of Black single mothers being poor or working class, living in low-income neighborhoods or homeless, and raising multiple children being "less than," other issues, such as those associated with mental health, substance use, domestic violence, and the like, may arise, further adding to the stigma experienced by these mothers.

Thoughtful Reflection

In what ways have you experienced ideological oppression . . .

Personally?

____

____

____

____

____

Professionally?

Addressing Ideological Oppression

As early as the 1990s, social workers began to look for ways to address oppression based on Eurocentric, patriarchic, and capitalist worldviews by implementing Africentrism in social work practice (Murphy et al., 2009). Once again, we see scholars suggesting that this practice arose from the identification of "services and practices for child welfare [being] historically designed using models that pathologize and devalue the unique cultural attributes of African Americans" (Murphy et al., 2009, p. 33). The shortcoming of the child welfare system is the continual misunderstanding of the impact of a long history of racism and sexism on the outcomes of Black single mothers. Too often, policies and procedures are based on the ideas that racism is a thing of the past, that there is an abundance of opportunities for anyone who is willing to put in hard work, and that any differences between the races are related to the poor moral character of the individual and the collective shortcomings of their race, not the ideological oppression that underlies their discriminatory experience.

According to Hill (2001), "Black families clearly value children, and through a unique dual socialization process attempt to pass on to them a combination of American and African based values" (p. 495). Honoring and respecting this dual socialization is the first key for social workers to address the negative ideas that continue the experience of oppression. Practitioners must understand that the makeup of the Black family began with women as the head of the household prior to slaves being brought to the United States and being introduced to the family structure of slave owners.

Additionally, social workers must work to identify their own biases and how those biases impact their work with Black single mothers. Because this level oppression goes beyond the thoughts and feelings of the individual, and is specifically focused on a widespread historical ideology that has been accepted by the vast majority, social workers must seek to step into their roles as change agents to radically address and ameliorate all forms of oppression from the top down.

Social workers should also work to understand the stigma faced by individuals within the Black community who receive services such as counseling or substance use treatment or who are involved in domestic violence programs. Within the broad culture of the Black family, these areas of concern should be addressed either solely by the family or by turning to the family's religious faith. Here, it is key for child welfare social workers to think beyond completing referrals to mental health treatment providers or other community entities and to also include the family's informal support system—extended family, religious entities, and fictive kin.

Institutional and Structural Oppression

Sanctions to Temporary Assistance for Needy Families and reproductive justice arguments suggesting single women should delay childbearing until after marriage or those on welfare should cease to have children until they are able to support their children without public assistance are glaring examples of institutional and structural oppression. With the understanding that each facet of oppression builds upon the one before it, institutional oppression becomes the operationalizing of racial and gender ideology. According to Neville and Hamer (2001), institutional and structural oppression presents as "the systems in which society is organized, including political, economic, and social institutions" (p. 441). As has been noted, poor and working-class Black women experience both institutional and structural oppression due to their race, class, and gender. Not only are these women readily targeted for economic exploitation, they are also the most distanced from positions of power and control. "Institutional racism has been identified as one of the key factors in the continued oppression of Black families within society" (Graham, 1999, p. 104), and its effects permeate socioeconomic status, neighborhood composition, media portrayals of Black single mothers, politics, and practices of the social and child welfare systems.

Socioeconomic Disadvantages

Both sexism and racism have greatly contributed to the lack of employment opportunities for Black single mothers that will raise them above the poverty line. Over time, forms of employment have become both racial and gender based. In today's society, there are jobs deemed as men's work and others deemed as women's work. Those positions deemed as men's work come with higher pay, but not necessarily greater responsibility, whereas women are being paid less for similar work. Racially speaking, Black women are "relegated to the very lowest paying and lowest quality positions" (Neville & Hamer, 2001, p. 442), thus leaving them vulnerable to remaining below or at the poverty line.

The structure of the U.S. workforce has changed over the past decade to a labor market offering part-time, temporary, low-wage positions. Women, and women of color in particular, tend to be disproportionately represented in these positions. Black single mothers who are the heads of their households are less likely to be employed due to the demands of single parenthood. Additionally, due to the income requirements and cutoffs, Black single mothers are choosing not to enter the workforce, as this will directly affect the amount of public assistance they receive, because the slight increase in wage income does not make up for the amount of assistance lost.

Neighborhood Composition and Effects

The segregation of neighborhoods dates back to the 1950s and the time of "white flight" when White families moved from the inner cities to the suburbs in response to Black families being granted the right to own land. Many neighborhoods continue to be segregated today. Poor Black families find themselves residing in hypersegregated, deprived, and isolated communities as a result of various institutional-level oppressions. For the past 60 years, federal lending policy has worked to the advantage of White families, while regularly denying Black families the opportunity to obtain funds to purchase homes in the suburbs. Connected to this was the use of transportation funding to build roads into the suburbs rather than providing improved public transit within the city. Additionally, real estate brokers and mortgage lenders would specifically only show Black families homes in Black neighborhoods, thereby maintaining segregation. This segregation was then enforced by zoning and the almost impossible feat for Black families to obtain lines of credit. To add to this, Black families found themselves isolated from banks, thus having to give a percentage of their wages to check-cashing establishments. The lack of employment led to a drop in property values due to increased illegal activity and a decline in the security of these inner-city neighborhoods (Miller & Garran, 2007). Further, there is also evidence to suggest that some employers avoid hiring Black women who reside in predominantly Black areas or those who are perceived to be public assistance recipients (Neville & Hamer, 2001).

Media Portrayal

The media, whether it be television, music videos, news broadcasts, newspapers, editorial magazines, or scholarly journals, continue to expose society to specific images that uphold the ideology of the dominant group. Stereotypes are often ingrained through cultural upbringing, but these stereotypes are then upheld through what is seen on television or the Internet. "Throughout life people are continually bombarded by complimentary narratives" (Miller & Garran, 2007, p. 59) that present White women as the heroines, decision makers, and leaders, while Black women are typically portrayed as housekeepers, loud and obnoxious, or fully sexualized beings (Miller & Garran, 2007). As described in an earlier chapter, a number of stereotypes have been placed on Black single mothers since the antebellum era that suggest that they alone are the cause of the downfall of Black culture. Unfortunately, these stereotypes are still carried out today in the media, from as far back as President Ronald Reagan and his portrayal of a Black welfare queen, to today with Black women being hypersexualized based on the shape of their bodies. As will be discussed later, these portrayals have become commonplace within the Black community as a marker of internalized oppression.

Political Incorporation of Oppression

Political incorporation of oppression speaks to the basis and foundation of racist and sexist legislation that is developed and ultimately passed based on the ideal presented previously. In the United States, those who are able to make political decisions are seen as the people who have power. Over the course of history, politicians have been White males of affluence. These White males bring with them ideals and beliefs regarding women, Black men, and Black women. As they move into positions of power, these ideals are then integrated into the legislation that is ultimately voted on and pushed forward. This is how the conceptualization of racial and gender-based ideologies is operationalized and spread throughout the nation's culture. The purpose of this text is not to delve into the processes of how legislation is passed or how new guidelines and processes are set in place, but rather to focus on those laws, practices, and amendments that continue to place Black single mothers in a position of subordination rather than uplift.

Recall the discussion of the history of the child welfare system in Chapter One. Black children were essentially ignored in our nation's early history as being dependent and in need of fostering-type care. Instead, during the time of slavery, these children were often sold away from their mothers, and once slavery ended, they became indentured servants. Upon the abolishment of slavery, Black mothers found themselves having to fight to be seen as the legal custodians or guardians over their own children. These practices spoke to the laws at the time that left Black people as property. These types of laws, which left Black single mothers in precarious situations, continued to develop throughout history. Consider voting rights for women, a lack of Black male representation in political roles until 1928, and Black female representation decades later. This history laid the foundation for racist and sexist legislation to be passed at the federal level that continues the oppression of Black single mothers.

Those in political power are seen as role models and basically set the tone for how people in power should treat others. These leaders over time have set the tone for racist and sexist ideas as being acceptable. Miller and Garran (2007) conclude that these individuals are "highly visible opinion shapers in what becomes a public discourse that no longer is concerned about racism and inequities, but instead emphasizes how people of color 'cheat the system'" (p. 58).

By upholding the damaging stereotypes of Black single mothers presented earlier, politicians and lawmakers deemed it necessary to control the fertility and reproduction rates of poor women. This was presented in such a way as to limit taxpayer money from being used to care for children who were brought into the world by single mothers who ultimately could not provide for them. Currently, legislators in a number of states are diligently working towards passing legislation requiring family planning services as a prerequisite for some single mothers to receive or continue to receive public assistance (Thomas, 1998). Table 3.1 lists a number of eugenic sterilization laws that have been proposed or passed.

Table 3.1 **Eugenic Sterilization Legislation**

Legislation	*Year*	*Description*
Model Eugenical Sterilization Law	1914	Authorized sterilization of the "socially inadequate," the "feebleminded, insane, criminalistic, epileptic, inebriate, diseased, blind, deaf; deformed; and dependent," including "orphans, ne'er-do-wells, tramps, the homeless and paupers" (Lombardo, 2015, para. 2).
Eugenical Sterilization Act	1924	• Adopted as part of a cost-saving strategy to relieve the tax burden in a state where public facilities for the "insane" and "feebleminded" had experienced rapid growth. • Protected physicians who performed sterilizing operations from malpractice lawsuits. • Focused on "defective persons" whose reproduction represented "a menace to society" (Lombardo, 2015, para. 3).
The 1930s saw an increase of the number of women being sterilized, but by the 1940s many states discontinued this practice. However, by the 1950s and 1960s there was an increase in the number of Black women receiving Aid to Dependent Children, taking taxpayer funds away from "deserving widows."		
Eugenic Sterilization Law	1957	Required forced sterilization of welfare mothers, with the underlying assumption that "poverty, illegitimacy, and welfare dependence were 'Negro Problems' that threatened the White race" (Thomas, 1998, p. 424).
An Act to Discourage Immorality of Unmarried Females by Providing for the Sterilization of the Unwed Mother Under Conditions of this Act and for Related Purposes	1958	Allowed court proceedings against single mothers who gave birth to additional children while receiving public assistance. If it was determined the mother's moral character threatened the community, she was sterilized. This bill was defended by lawmakers as the bill would stop childbearing among the Black population.

(Continued)

Table 3.1 **(Continued)**

Legislation	*Year*	*Description*
Again, although the above bills did not become laws, they spoke to the underlying ideological oppression that was infused into the political arena. There was a brief pause in these sterilization reforms; however, in the 1990s the conversation around an increase in births to single mothers began discussion on controlling women's fertility once again.		
Parental and Family Responsibility Act	1992	A sort of child disincentive act that imposed a strict one-child-per-family cap on AFDC benefits.

Table 3.1 brings us to more recent legislation introduced in 1996. The Personal Responsibility and Work Opportunity Reconciliation Act of 1996 replaced Aid to Families with Dependent Children (AFDC) with a state-level block grant program, or Temporary Assistance to Needy Families (TANF). TANF was presented as a way to move needy families away from receiving cash benefits to a welfare-to-work program. Additional major changes of this program included the introduction of lifetime limits on receiving welfare benefits, strict guidelines for work, and educational/vocational program attendance requirements. States were given flexibility to determine how these changes would be implemented. TANF places a 5-year time limit on cash assistance and does not guarantee employment or some level of wage once this time limit has been reached. With the ability to maintain flexibility in implementing this reform, states were granted permission from the federal government to implement sanctions.

Sanctions are the consequences of adult recipients not complying with work/education requirements, not cooperating with child support enforcement, missing appointments, and, in some cases, "not following rules." These sanctions can be imposed as full loss of benefits or partial loss of benefits, at the discretion of the state. Several studies have shown a split between states determining if full sanctions will be the norm or if caseworkers are more willing to work with families through a partial sanction. Often, if a family has received a sanction and they are able to come into compliance within a set timeframe their benefits and support will be reinstated.

A study conducted by Cherlin, Bogen, Quane, and Burton (2002) identified the following reasons for sanctions:

- Missed appointments or paperwork problem (35%)
- Paperwork problem (21%)
- Work-related rule (11%)
- Failed to attend school (11%)
- Failed to comply with child support enforcement (10%)
- Child-related rule (6%)
- Other reason (9%)
- Recipient did not know why they were sanctioned or refused to provide this information (5%)

For clarity, the child-related rule is in regards to parents having their children immunized or to attending regular medical appointments and ensuring school attendance.

How is this reform to welfare oppressive? What has been seen in the research is that families who receive sanctions tend to have underlying issues that keep them from falling in line with the expectations of the system. These families tend to be "more vulnerable than other families, they have worse health (60%), lower levels of education (nearly half), more children in the household, and higher rates of domestic violence" (Monnat, 2010, p. 639), struggle with substance abuse (15–20%), have been victims of abuse (60%), and are living with mental health concerns (40%) (Neville & Hamer, 2001). More specifically, Black women find themselves receiving a higher rate of sanctions than others. Once sanctions are in place, these families have a more difficult time finding employment than those who continue receiving services through TANF.

Although this reform to the welfare system was intended to "reduce dependence on the government by changing the behavior of welfare recipients along several dimensions, including work, marriage, and childbearing" (Cherlin et al., 2002, p. 388), it has more or less placed an even greater burned on households headed by Black single mothers.

Institutional Processes

To this point, the focus of institutional oppression has been on socioeconomic factors, neighborhood composition, the media, and federal legislation that impacts Black single mothers across the spectrum. Institutional processes as they are related to institutional oppression focus on assessment and practices related to the child welfare system. As noted earlier, Black children are disproportionately involved with the child welfare system as compared to White children. Studies of the overrepresentation of Black families in child protection suggests that overrepresentation occurs due to racial discrimination not only on an interpersonal level, but also institutionally. Within each aspect of child protective services—investigations, in-home support services, or out-of-home care—assessment is the foundation for all decision making. These assessments are not solely up to the social worker's discretion, but are guided by evidence-based assessment tools. One concern that has arisen over the years is that these assessment tools are often made reliable based on the culture of the dominant society, thus perpetuating a level of homogeneity when it comes to family expectations within child welfare. In most cases, these assessments are focused on what have been deemed the basic needs of children. As presented in the British Department of Health's *Protecting Children: A Guide for Social Workers Undertaking a Comprehensive Assessment* (1988), these basic needs are:

1 Physical care
2 Affection
3 Security
4 Stimulation of innate potential
5 Guidance and control

6 Responsibility
7 Independence

Each of these dimensions parallel areas of care and protection that are also assessed throughout the United States by child welfare agencies. The concern here is that many of these dimensions come with objective, rather than subjective, evidence. Who is to say that a parent living in abject poverty is not still providing for the physical care, security, and guidance of her child? How can these dimensions truly be operationalized in such a way as to be assessed equally across race, class, and gender?

It is clear that there will be a higher representation of Black children and families being assessed across these domains. Not only that, but because of stereotypes of Black single mothers' abilities and motives and cultural differences in childrearing, expectations will directly affect the outcome of child welfare assessments. A Black single mother's ability to provide for the physical care of her child will likely be impacted by access to affordable housing, under- or unemployment, and a lack of a social support system. "Any assessment process that sees these as the failing of Black people as indicators of child abuse rather than the effects of racial inequality is in itself is racist" (Chand, 2000, p. 73).

Thoughtful Reflection

Taking into consideration the seven dimensions of children's basic needs, what are ways in which Black single mothers meet these needs as compared to others? Additionally, what might be barriers to meeting these needs?

Physical Care

____

____

____

____

Affection

Security

Stimulation of Innate Potential

Guidance and Control

Responsibility

Independence

Truthfully, there is no right or wrong answer to these questions. The key in working with any family is to perform the assessment based on the family's experiences of the various levels of oppression that are beyond their control.

Institutional oppression through institutional processes also occurs through the use of evidence-based assessment tools to determine the likelihood of future maltreatment. One such tool that is used in several jurisdictions is the Structured Decision Making (SDM™) risk and safety assessment.

The National Council on Crime and Delinquency (2015) defines the SDM as a model for child protection agencies that assists workers in assessing and promoting child safety and well-being. It is a research- and evidence-based system designed to guide structured assessments to improve child welfare decisions. There are also service standards, guidelines for reassessments, and ways to ensure accountability and quality in child welfare work. Additionally, the tool supports the reduction of additional maltreatment and helps children reach permanency, whether through reunification or other means more quickly.

The SDM is set up in such a way that states and other child welfare agencies can tailor the tool to fit their needs. The SDM, like the British guide for social workers, assesses families in multiple areas. The SDM assesses three domains: child risk factors, parental/family risk factors, and social/environmental risk factors. The SDM is significant to this discussion because some areas of this assessment tend to be specific to the experience of Black single mothers.

The SDM tool assesses life circumstances, such as multiple reports to CPS, multiple children in the home, the age of the caregiver, and characteristics of the children. Delinquency, medically fragile, developmental disability, and substance use or mental health treatment history all suggest an increased level of neglect. For assessment of the risk for abuse, instances of domestic violence in the home, insufficient emotional/psychological support of the child from the caregiver, and prior childhood abuse history of the caregiver are taken into consideration.

The results of this assessment then determine if the family's case will be closed, opened for in-home services, or if the children cannot remain safely in the home. As noted throughout this text, Black single mothers are more likely to have multiple calls to child welfare agencies due to a lack of cultural competence in reporters, the differences between childrearing practices, and a lack of understanding of the cultural differences in how Black mothers respond to the emotional needs of their children. In the hands of a social worker who is unaware of the various barriers faced by Black single mothers, an assessment tool like the SDM will continually assess for moderate and high levels of risk that are not actually there.

Addressing Institutional Oppression

Black single mothers continually face obstacles that are beyond their control as a result of institutional oppression. These obstacles are deeply rooted in what society first believed Black single mothers to be capable of and then these oppressive beliefs were used as the foundation to develop practices and policies. Here, the idea of stepping into the role of being a radical social worker comes to light. Gil (2013) suggests that the goal of radical social work is "to transcend conventional social work practice and function as agents of social change," which requires "theoretical and philosophical perspectives and practice principles different from those now dominant in the profession" (p. 107).

The second key component to addressing institutional oppression is that child welfare social workers must remain diligent in understanding the impact of the policies and procedures outlined for them in their various practice models. When there is an opportunity to seek policy revisions or to ensure policy implementation that makes sense for all of their clients, social workers must see themselves as change agents and move away from checking boxes and meeting timeframes and benchmarks.

Finally, addressing institutional oppression means to consistently question the institution and its functions. Are the policies antiquated and based on assumptions from the beginning of child welfare history? Have policymakers taken into consideration the voices of not just those who are able to fund their cause, but those who will be directly affected by reforms? One key notion of social work is that social workers find themselves as the voice for the voiceless. Black single mothers may represent a significant portion of child welfare cases, but due to the constant devaluing and silencing of them as Black women, their voice is often unheard.

Thoughtful Reflection

The Singleton–Betts–Davidson Family (continued)

Reconsider the case example presented in Chapter Two about Ms. Singleton and her family. The following is additional information regarding her case:

> Based on the risk assessment completed by the investigative social worker and Ms. Singleton's previous history with the agency, it was determined that an in-home protective services case should be opened. Ms. Singleton would need to make herself and her children available to an in-home social worker at least two times per month and work with the social worker to develop a family case plan to address the concerns of the original report to CPS.
>
> Due to Ms. Singleton having four children, one of whom is under the age of 2 and another who is experiencing developmental disabilities; a previous history with CPS; Ms. Singleton having previous mental health treatment history, as well as previous marijuana use history; and being considered homeless at the time of the investigation, the risk assessment completed by the CPS social worker determined that her children were at a very high risk for future neglect.

In what ways have the concepts of ideological and institutional oppression played out for this family?

Ideological

___

___

___

___

___

Institutional

___

___

___

___

___

Interpersonal Oppression

Every day Black single mothers are faced with interpersonal oppression, the easiest and most visible of all types of oppression. This layer of oppression speaks directly to experiences of racism, sexism, and classism at the person-to-person level. It is seen in derogatory jokes, name-calling, and negative behaviors geared towards those who are being oppressed. Trickling down from ideological to institutional, interpersonal oppression means members of the dominant culture have been given permission to uphold the oppressive ideologies of the group.

Bonilla-Silva (2001) speaks of the concept of color-blind racism, or racism based on socially constructed ideologies. The three frames of color-blind racism are abstract liberalism, cultural racism, and minimization of racism and discrimination. Although, Bonilla-Silva does not speak to gender and class as a part of this concept, both can be readily folded into the definition.

Abstract liberalism speaks to the individuals who believe everyone has equal opportunity to employment, housing, social support, and the like, while ignoring the historical impact of oppression for these people. Abstract liberalism is often the foundation for the opposition of antiracist theories of social work practice and, more popularly, affirmative action efforts.

When individuals believe there is something inherently wrong with a culture's morals and values, they are in the midst of the frame of cultural racism. An example of cultural racism, and how sexism can be folded in, leads us back to the conversation of Black single mothers being touted as welfare queens. This moniker "invokes the image of the lazy, typically Black, mother on public assistance who deliberately breeds children at the expense of taxpayer" (Monnat, 2010, p. 643), which leads to the assumption that these mothers are living in poverty because of the number of children living with them.

Minimization of racism and discrimination is the point at which individuals of the majority suggest that racism, sexism, and classism do not in fact have a negative impact on the experiences of the subordinate group. These individuals hold fast to the belief that the history of Black single mothers in the United States is not relevant to their experiences today or that because the United States has had a Black president for the past two terms racism is no longer an issue.

In addition to this concept of color-blind racism, interpersonal oppression can be seen in the manner in which services are provided to Black single mothers. Research suggests that the racist, sexist, and classist beliefs of social workers, case managers, and other social service professionals directly impact the way in which these professionals not only provide services to Black single mothers, but also the quality of the services (Chand, 2000; Abrams & Curran, 2004; Watkins-Hayes, 2009). According to Watkins-Hayes (2009), "Caseworkers have been known to exercise power through their interactions with clients in ways that define the terms of citizenship vis-à-vis access to public resources, enforce certain interpretations of social rights and obligations, make moral assertions about the poor . . . and perpetuate interracial inequalities" (p. 286).

Classism is also a form of interpersonal oppression that can be seen through relationships between child welfare social workers and Black single mothers. Oftentimes, child welfare social workers are in a different socioeconomic class than the families with whom they work. Classism speaks to prejudice one social class may have against another. This issue of classism may arise when Black single mothers work with Black social workers. Black social workers may lack an understanding of the oppression faced by Black single mothers, because they themselves were able to access education, and ultimately sustainable employment.

Fletcher (1997) discusses the concept of emic perspective: "An emic perspective includes a structural understanding of social systems as well as highly specific cultural knowledge, self-awareness, and interpretations pertaining to . . . a group's worldview" (p. 215). For Black social workers working with Black single mothers, there is a level of emic perspective that leads to assumptions about racism, injustice, and oppression. There may be times, based on these assumptions, when Black social workers find it difficult to manage their own response to oppressive experiences in order to be most effective with their Black clients, particularly if the social worker holds to the ideas of the dominant culture regarding the involvement of Black single mothers with the welfare system.

Another way interpersonal oppression occurs in social worker–client relationships is through microaggressions: "Microaggressions are subtle insults (verbal, nonverbal, and/or visual) directed toward people of color, often automatically or unconsciously" (Solorazano, Ceja, & Yosso, 2000, p. 60). According to Pierce (1995), "In and of itself a microaggression may seem harmless, but the cumulative burden of a lifetime of microaggressions can theoretically contribute to diminished mortality, augmented morbidity, and flattened confidence" (p. 281).

Thoughtful Reflection: Everyday Microaggressions

"You're cute for a Black girl."
"When I talk about 'those people,' I don't mean you!"
"I don't see you as Black."

"She is so articulate" (in reference to a Black woman).
"What are their father's names?" (To a Black woman, assuming her children have different fathers).

Considering this list, what are some microaggressions you have committed? How could you rephrase these statements to be more culturally sensitive?

Addressing Interpersonal Oppression

Chand (2000) postulates that if a social worker holds the belief that Black single mothers are inferior or that all families should be treated the same, then these families will be at a disadvantage on some level because all facets of their oppression, and ultimately their involvement in child welfare, will not be addressed. Therefore, it is the responsibility of social workers to harbor a level of self-awareness, understand the impact of microaggressions, and ultimately accept that to some extent everyone holds prejudice.

Although receiving some knowledge about a specific culture through cultural competency training can place a social worker in a better position to address interpersonal oppression, this type of training can also give the social worker a false sense of security. By attending cultural competency training, social workers may feel that they have a full understanding of a culture different from their own and may enter into working relationships with families and unknowingly offend them, which damages the working relationship. Again, self-awareness and realizing that everything about every culture cannot be known will help the social worker to address this level of oppression.

Internalized Oppression

"It is a peculiar sensation, this double-consciousness, this sense of always looking at one's self through the eyes of others, of measuring one's soul by the tape of a world that looks on in amused contempt and pity" (DuBois, 1903, quoted in Pyke, 2010, p. 551).

Internalized oppression is the "individual inculcation of racist stereotypes, values, images, and ideologies perpetuated by the White dominant society about one's racial group leading to feelings of self-doubt, disgust, and disrespect for one one's race and/or oneself" (Pyke, 2010, p. 553). This oppression can be seen in the ways Black single mothers talk about themselves or how high they set their self-expectations. These women are faced with judgment, disdain, and direct hate from many directions. They are put in a position that sets them up to begin to internalize the racial and gender ideologies that have permeated the institutions they must work with due to the ideas that they are less than anyone else who may be living in poverty, struggling with mental health issues, or are being faced with separation from their children.

A study conducted by Szymanski and Stewart (2010) "indicated that when examined separately, greater frequency of perceived experiences of racist and sexist events are related to greater psychological distress for African American women" (p. 234). Further, this study found a correlation between perceived experiences of sexist events and psychological distress. This is explained as one's minority identity being influenced by identifying with the minority group as well as feeling different from the minority group. Black women may be accepted by Black men on a racial level but shunned due to gender, and accepted by White women based on gender but shunned due to race (Szymanski & Stewart, 2010).

In addition to addressing their own internalized oppression, Black single mothers are also faced with supporting their children through their experience. Bernard (2002) states "it is argued that Black children may have difficulties unraveling whether their feelings of worthlessness may be due to the abuse they have experienced or the pervasive effects of racism" (p. 241). It has been further suggested that Black children, as all children, may internalize their experiences of abuse as being solely related to personal attributes and not an understanding of the parents' own frustration either with their current situation or lack of coping skills.

Addressing Internalized Oppression

Black single mothers must be given the space to develop new self-narratives. They must be allowed to uncover the internal wounds of oppression through individual counseling, group work, pastoral counseling, and through the same self-care techniques taught to social workers throughout their careers. Until Black single mothers are given the space to heal from the internalized oppression they experience, they will not be able to move into a place of enhancing parenting, obtaining viable employment, and ensuring the safety, permanence, and well-being of their children.

Ponds (2013) suggests that the experience of racism, and ultimately oppression, leads to an experience of trauma. "Racism maintains domination, power, and control . . . the basis of trauma" (p. 23). Racial trauma is the damage that is done to a person's physiology, psyche, and emotional well-being that leads to a level of distress and, in severe cases, disorders. Once the individual begins to turn on themselves because of the inundation of the ideals of the oppressive majority, there is a new level of trauma to address. It may be necessary for social workers to move away from focusing on the presenting problem while disregarding the racial trauma. With this in mind, trauma therapy may be a necessary key in addressing internalized oppression as well.

Thoughtful Reflection

In what ways might internalized oppression manifest in families involved with the child welfare system?

Removing the Weight of Oppression

The four layers of oppression cause a heavy weight on those who are experiencing oppression. This weight can become heavier as individuals age and continue to experience oppression and as their psyche begins to absorb the ideals that are the basis of oppression. In order for this weight to be lifted and for oppression to be addressed effectively, it is necessary to address each layer through a bottom-up approach. Not particularly in regards to the conversation of oppression, Alexander-Floyd (2012) writes, "Black women who are multiply challenged confront a bottom-up reality, fighting through layers of harms not easily deduced to either race or gender" (p. 7). There is easily a comparison between the weight of racism, sexism, antinatalism, and other stigmas placed on Black single mothers involved with the child welfare system and understanding the need to address the layers of harm placed on those mothers who are not involved with child welfare.

Oppression must be understood from a bottom-up approach. To eradicate the effects of oppression, social workers must work in such a way as to address the negative images, thoughts, and feelings their clients feel about themselves based on the oppression they have faced from others and the institutions they interact with that are governed by policies shaped by oppressive ideals. Then their work must focus on the racism, sexism, and classism that occurs from one individual to the next. The bigger task then becomes addressing policies and procedures that act as oppressive forces to Black single mothers being able to see and feel child welfare success. Finally, and likely the most difficult to achieve, child welfare social workers must work to challenge the oppressive ideals of those who maintain the power to make reform decisions—agency directors and administrators, commissioners, mayors, voters, and policymakers.

Privilege

A discussion of oppression would not be complete without defining privilege and understanding its basis and conditions. Privilege, over time, has been a difficult concept for many to grasp in light of discussions on racism, sexism, classism, and other types of oppression. The first key to understanding privilege is understanding that to some extent every individual experiences privilege. Whether the privilege is access to education; being able-bodied; or being able to read, write, and speak the language of the dominant culture, privilege is to individuals as strengths are to children, youth, and families involved with the child welfare system.

One source defines privilege as "unearned advantages enjoyed by a particular group simply because of membership in that group" (Swigonski, 1996, p. 153). Further, "privileges accrue to those who (consciously or not) oppress others and are general invisible to those who enjoy them" (p. 153). The basis of privilege is found in the history of the United States and the development of the layers of oppression. Theorists have identified 54 conditions of privilege that "invisibly permeate the mundane activities of daily life yet significantly influence the texture of one's existence" (p. 154). An understanding of these 54 conditions is not necessary, but knowledge of the fact they exist is key: "For members of marginalized groups, awareness of difference and awareness of privilege are needed for survival" (Swigonski, 1996, p. 155).

Privilege and the Game of Monopoly

The following vignette was inspired by a presentation on race presented at the University of Wisconsin by Allan Johnson (2012).

It's a Friday night, and you are ready to have family game night, and tonight's game of choice is Monopoly. You know the game; your sister is always the banker, your brother is always the first one to buy property. This game lasts for hours and can get quite ruthless.

You've now been playing this game for an hour. Your brother has all the dark blue properties and has outfitted each with hotels. You have had the opportunity to purchase all the utilities and the railroads. When anyone lands on your properties they must pay you rent.

You and the family are now at the beginning of the second hour of the game and there's a knock at the door. Your cousins who live a few cities over have decided to come and join the fun game, but your family is too far in to start over. As your cousins sit down to play it becomes evident that all the sought-after properties have been purchased and they now only have the option of renting. There was not enough money in the bank at this point to deal them in for the full $1,500, and therefore they had to settle for $500 apiece. No matter how much of a champion Monopoly player your cousin is or how strategically either plays the game, neither is able to reach the level of your immediate family financially or in land ownership.

Privilege is like this. For centuries White men were playing the game until women were given the right to vote and slaves were freed. These marginalized groups were dealt into the game centuries after land was already purchased and financial resources divvied up equally. These groups were forced to settle for what was left over. No matter how diligently these groups work, regardless of educational status or employment status, it is nearly impossible for them to catch up to those who have had the power all along.

Thoughtful Reflection

Considering the definition of privilege presented in the text, what are your privileges?

References

Abrams, L., & Curran, L. (2004). Between women: Gender and social work in historical perspective. *Social Service Review, 78*(3), 429–446.

Alexander-Floyd, N. (2012). Disappearing acts: Reclaiming intersectionality in the social sciences in a post-Black feminist era. *Feminist Formations, 24*(1), 1–25.

Bernard, C. (2002). Giving voice to experiences: Parental maltreatment of black children in the context of societal racism. *Child and Family Social Work, 7*, 239–251.

Bonilla-Silva, E. (2001). *White supremacy and racism in the post-civil rights era.* Boulder, CO: Lynne Rienner.

Chand, A. (2000). The over-representation of Black children in the child protection system: Possible causes, consequences and solutions. *Child and Family Social Work, 5*, 67–77.

Cherlin, A., Bogen, K., Quane, J., & Burton, J. (2002). Operating within the rules: Welfare recipients' experiences with sanctions and case closings. *Social Service Review, 76*(3), 387–405.

Department of Health. (1988). *Protecting children: A guide for social workers undertaking a comprehensive assessment.* London: HMSO.

DuBois, W.E.B. (1903). *The souls of Black folks.* Chicago, IL: University Press.

Fletcher, B. (1997). Same-race practice: Do we expect too much or too little? *Child Welfare, 76*(1), 213–237.

Gamst, G., Der-Karabetian, A, & Dane, R. (2008). *Readings in multicultural practice.* Los Angeles, CA: SAGE Publications.
Gil, D.G. (2013). *Confronting injustice and oppression: Concepts and strategies for social workers.* New York, NY: Columbia University Press.
Goldenberg, I. (1978). *Oppression and social intervention.* Chicago, IL: Nelson-Hall.
Graham, M. (1999). The African-centered worldview: Toward a paradigm for social work. *Journal of Black Studies, 30*(1), 103–122.
Hill, S.A. (2001). Class, race, and gender dimensions of child rearing in African American families. *Journal of Black Studies, 31*(4), 494–508.
Johnson, A. (2012). People, systems, and the game of monopoly. Presentation at the University of Wisconsin. Retrieved April 20, 2015, from www.agjohnson.us/audiovideo/monopoly/
Lombardo, P. (2015). *Eugenic sterilization laws.* Retrieved from http://www.eugenicsarchive.org/html/eugenics/essay8text.html
Miller, J., & Garran, A.M. (2007). The web of institutional racism. *Smith College Studies in Social Work, 77*(1), 33–68.
Monnat, S. (2010). Toward a critical understanding of gendered color-blind racism within the US welfare institution. *Journal of Black Studies, 40*(4), 637–652.
Murphy, Y., Hunt, V., Zajicek, A., Norris, A., & Hamilton, L. (2009). *Incorporating intersectionality in social work practice, research, policy, and education.* Washington, DC: NASW Press.
National Council on Crime and Delinquency (2015). The Structured Decision Making® (SDM) model in child protection. Retrieved April 30, 2015, from http://www.nccdglobal.org/assessment/sdm-structured-decision-making-systems/child-welfare
Neville, H., & Hamer, J. (2001). We make freedom: An exploration of revolutionary Black feminism. *Journal of Black Studies, 31*(4), 437–461.
Pierce, C. (1995). Stress analogs of racism and sexism: Terrorism, torture, and disaster. In C. Willie, P. Rieker, B. Kramer, and B. Brown (eds.), *Mental health, racism, and sexism* (pp. 277–293). Pittsburgh: University of Pittsburgh Press.
Ponds, K. (2013). The trauma of racism: America's original sin. *Reclaiming Children and Youth, 22*(2), 22–24.
Pyke, K.D. (2010). What is internalized oppression and why don't we study it? Acknowledging racism's hidden injuries. *Sociological Perspectives, 53*(4), 551–572.
Roberts, D. (1997). Unshackling Black motherhood. *Michigan Law Review, 95*(4), 938–964.
Solorazano, D., Ceja, M., & Yosso, T. (2000). Critical race theory, racial microaggressions, and campus racial climate: The experiences of African American College Students. *The Journal of Negro Education, 69*(1/2), 60–73.
Swigonski, M.E. (1996). Challenging privilege through Africentric social work practice. *Social Work, 41*(2), 153–161.

Szymanski, D., & Stewart, D. (2010). Racism and sexism as correlates of African American women's psychological distress. *Sex Roles, 63*, 226–238.

Thomas, S. (1998). Race, gender, and welfare reform: The antinatalist response. *Journal of Black Studies, 28*(4), 419–446.

Watkins-Hayes, C. (2009). Race-ing the bootstrap climb: Black and Latino bureaucrats in post-reform welfare offices. *Social Problems, 56*(2), 285–310.

4

TRANSFORMING CHILD WELFARE

The final chapter of this handbook focuses on transforming child welfare to address the unique and specific needs of Black single mothers who are involved with this system. This chapter will provide a compilation of various theories used throughout the social sciences in an effort to reintroduce child welfare social workers and professionals to the social work profession and introduce ways to incorporate the old with the new.

This chapter does not seek to provide an exhaustive detailing of various theories, and it is highly recommended that the reader seek out the theorists and researchers mentioned for greater detail. Here is the opportunity to spark interest in the topic and to support social workers in rekindling their passion and excitement for the profession.

Thoughtful Reflection

As a social worker, it is easy to get lost in the bureaucracy of what it means to meet the varied needs of the families and children with whom you work in the midst of meeting specific benchmarks or agency expectations and goals.

The longer social workers are "in the field," the farther away from their passion they may find themselves. Rarely do social workers have the opportunity to recall and reflect upon the reasons they have entered into this profession.

Prior to reviewing this chapter, take a minute or two to think back to the moment you decided to study social work, and then take another minute to consider what keeps you practicing every day.

Why is this chapter titled "Transforming Child Welfare"? What does that mean? Why not seek to reform the system through federal legislation and public policy?

Dr. Trace Pickering (2011) discusses viewing various YouTube videos of the "late, great Russell Ackoff" in an effort to better understand the difference between transformation and reformation. Throughout the course of the social sciences, political science, medical science, and basically all knowledge bases "efforts at improvement and change are reformational in nature" (p. 1); that is to say, reformation attempts to change behaviors within the system. In contrast, transformation is the effort placed in changing a system's means to an ends, or its goals (see Table 4.1).

Table 4.1 **Transformation vs Reformation**

Reformation	*Transformation*
"to leave a system as it is and try to change its behavior through a modification of the means it employs."	"to change a system's objectives or ends and the means it employs to achieve those ends."

Robert Ackoff, as quoted in Pickering (2011).

Continue reviewing, reflecting, and absorbing the information in this chapter with these definitions and distinctions in mind.

Social Justice in Social Work

Social justice is a term that has been used throughout the history of social work to refer to social workers addressing oppression and other issues of human rights through implementing change. Social workers are often referred to as *change agents*; "They are charged with making change not only in the lives of the clients but in the micro, mezzo, and macro systems in which they work" (Murphy et al., 2009, p. 47). Social justice is broad term, much like oppression, intersectionality, and privilege, and little effort has been made to build it up as a concept. In a study by Vincent (2012), an attempt was made to conceptualize the term. Here, social justice was defined within the framework of three themes: distributive perspectives, relational/processional perspectives, and Sen's (2009) theory of social justice.

Distributive perspectives focus on distributing resources in an equitable manner (Vincent, 2012). This means reviewing federal and local policy to determine how resources can be divvied up in such a way that everyone involved benefits. As discussed throughout the text, Black single mothers tend to receive fewer benefits in the areas of education, employment, housing, and social services.

Relational/processional perspectives highlight the "interaction among dominant and minority groups and the societal process that lead to structural inequalities among these groups" (Vincent, 2012, p. 215). This is about addressing social constructs that highlight the dominance of White able-bodied heterosexual middle-class males and endorses "valuing human rights, individual/group rights, economic equity, and basic human dignity" (Vincent, 2012, p. 215).

Sen's (2009) theory focuses on the balance of two terms, equity and equality, and the absence of oppression at all levels. Equity is providing resources and support in an equal, fair, and impartial manner. Equality means to provide resources equally as it relates to a person or group's status, rights, and opportunities.

National Association of Social Workers (NASW) Code of Ethics

The National Association of Social Workers (NASW) is the governing body of the field of social work and was instrumental in social work being identified as a profession. The NASW has a widely accepted code of ethics that guides the ethical practice of social workers across the nation. As presented previously, social justice is one of the key values of the field of social work; thus, there are specific ethical guidelines and expectations for social workers. Recognizing that achieving social justice is about going beyond individual experiences and understanding history, community, and societal factors, the NASW identifies the following four social justice principles, as outlined in Austin (2014):

Principle 1: Partnership with and Advocacy on Behalf of Clients
Principle 2: Promotion of Cultural Competency and Equity
Principle 3: Opposition to Injustice and the Promotion of Empowerment and Equal Access
Principle 4: Advocacy for Environments Conducive to Social Justice

Council on Social Work Education (CSWE)

The Council on Social Work Education (CSWE) is the accrediting body for schools of social work nationally. It sets Educational Policy and Accreditation Standards (EPAS) for these schools based on the NASW Code of Ethics. In regards to social justice, the CSWE (2015) requires accredited schools to offer the following:

> *Social workers understand that every person regardless of position in society has fundamental human rights such as freedom, safety, privacy, an adequate standard of living, health care, and education.*

> *Social workers understand the global interconnections of oppression and human rights violations, and are knowledgeable about theories of justice and strategies to promote social justice and human rights. Social workers understand strategies designed to eliminate oppressive structural barriers to ensure that fundamental human rights are distributed equitably and without prejudice. Social workers:*
>
> - *apply their understanding of social justice to advocate for human rights; and*
> - *engage in practices that advance social and economic justice.*
>
> (p. 5)

Social Justice in Action

Social Intervention

In 1978, Ira Goldenberg discussed the concept of social intervention and its dimensions. He went further with this definition by laying out how social intervention occurs through three types of change agents.

Goldenberg (1978) suggested that an understanding of the term *social intervention* required a breakdown of the words *social* and *intervention*. *Social* is described as being reserved for "actions that are both collective in nature and oriented toward broad institutional policies rather than the individuals temporarily empowered to carry those policies" (p. 17). *Intervention* then "involves interference with an ongoing and often accepted social process" (p. 17). Therefore, social intervention means interfering with the accepted processes of institutions that seek to make policy changes on behalf of an oppressed group. To carry these changes out, Goldenberg (1978) introduces five dimensions. These dimensions are listed below, along with questions for self-reflection, which are a key concept in the practice of social work:

1 Degree of identification with the setting's underlying goals, assumptions, and intentions
  - Do my personal values and beliefs align with that of the system in which change is sought?

2 Belief in the need for basic systemic change
   - Is significant change needed in the structure of this system?

3 Source of agency
   - Whose change agent am I? Which group's interests are advanced by my behavior?

4 Problem of process
   - How can I support those being oppressed by the system to understand the personal, interpersonal, and/or intragroup dynamics that define some of their problems?

Note that individuals living under an oppressive state often do not often understand the impact of the four layers of oppression. In order to be most effective, an agent of change seeks to educate.

5 Belief in the changeability of the system through essentially peaceful means
   - Do I believe this level of change is possible without some level of violence (i.e. "total dismantling of existing institutional structures," Goldenberg, 1978, pp. 18–21).

To continue the discussion further, four types of individuals are involved in social intervention. First, the *social technician* is basically responsible for maintaining the status quo of the system. This individual often works from the space of abstract liberalism and strongly identifies with the values of the system and does not see a need for change.

Second, the *traditional social reformer* seeks to bridge the gap of misunderstanding between the oppressor and the oppressed. This individual works from the perspective of time, patience, and education being the catalysts of change.

Third, the *social interventionist* focuses on changing the ideologies that are upheld by the system that lead to oppression.

This individual "views the problem of basic institutional change as necessarily involving conflict and organization" (Goldenberg, 1978, p. 24).

Fourth, the *social revolutionary* seeks change with the assumption that peaceful transitions of power may not be possible due to historical imperatives. This individual approaches change stressing the "unalterable opposition of social groups" (Goldenberg, 1978, p. 25).

Radical Social Work

David Gil (2013) outlines principles of radical social work practice in the newest revision of his book *Confronting Oppression and Injustice*. These principles are:

- Rejecting political neutrality and affirming politics of social justice and human liberation
- Affirming values
- Transcending technical/professional approaches
- Facilitating critical consciousness through dialogue
- Advocating for human rights
- Gaining insight into personal oppression
- Prefiguring future possibilities
- Spreading critical consciousness and building social movements

In comparing the above list and the tenets of social intervention postulated by Goldenberg (1978), many similarities can be identified. Social justice is about being self-aware of personal bias and prejudice, as well as understanding how oppression has directly affected the social worker. Next, social justice seeks to listen to the experiences of the oppressed and identify ways in which these experiences can be addressed and brought to light.

Gil goes further, defining the characteristics of radical social workers, specifically those involved in child welfare. According to Gil (2013), radical social workers in child welfare "understand child abuse as 'counterviolence' by troubled parents and caregivers" (p. 116). Counterviolence is the notion of combating what Gil calls "societal violence" by reacting to violence with violence. Radical social workers do not support abusive or neglectful acts; however, they do have an understanding of the factors that underlie these acts. These social workers are concerned with the safety, permanence, and well-being of children and the entire family, including perpetrators of abuse/neglect. It is key to understand that radical social workers work with parents by first highlighting the parents' feelings towards their children and involvement with child welfare prior to addressing the presenting allegations. The strengths-based perspective is utilized to highlight the parents' strengths as well as their protective capacities (Gil, 2013). Protective capacities are those behaviors parents are able to put in place immediately to address concerns of safety. Strengths are innate characteristics that act as motivation for protective capacities. It is a strength for a mother to love her children; it is a protective capacity to use that love to identify appropriate adult supervision for her child while she is attending a job interview.

By working in this manner, radical social workers have the potential to decrease Black single mothers' ambivalence, fear, and resistance to working with the very system that historically has been the cause of their oppression. The underlying goal of social justice is to move to a place of advocacy for equal human rights and ultimately to becoming an ally to the oppressed.

Becoming an Ally

An *ally* is defined as "a member of an oppressor group who works to end a form of oppression which gives her or him privilege" (Bishop, 2002, p. 152). In her text, *Becoming an Ally* (2002), Bishop speaks to the steps to becoming an ally to the oppressed: understanding oppression, understanding different types of oppressions, seeking consciousness and healing, becoming a worker in one's own liberation, and, finally, becoming an ally. It is suggested that a person will know when he or she has reached the space of becoming an ally when the following characteristics are in place (Bishop, 2002):

- A sense of connection with other people
- An understanding of the concept of social structures and collective responsibility and therefore a lack of an individualistic stance and ego
- A sense of the process of change
- An understanding of their own process of learning
- A comprehension of "power-with" rather than "power-over"
- Honesty, openness, and lack of shame about personal limitations
- A knowledge and sense of history
- An acceptance of struggle and its facets
- An understanding of the ineffectiveness of good intentions if action is not taken
- A knowledge of personal roots

Thoughtful Reflection

Considering the lists of characteristics of radical social change agent social workers, in what ways have you been a radical change agent in your social work practice? What strategy or strategies have worked best for you?

Theoretical Perspectives

Currently, child welfare practice is guided by stringent guidelines based on evidence-based research in an effort to "increase the accountability and effectiveness of child protection work" (Davies & Collings, 2008, p. 8). The shift to this approach has been a response to child protection agencies across the country falling under the oversight of courts via consent decrees, and in some cases of receivership. There has also been the inclusion of antioppressive theories in addressing the needs of children, youth, and families involved in the child protection. These two approaches tend to be technical and analyze power dynamics and institutional oppression, moving away from a focus on the underlying issues of the other layers of oppression. Thus, social work has shifted away from accepting the importance of the social worker–client relationship towards a more rational and technical approach to practice. According to Davies and Collings (2008), "Child protection practice has come to rely almost exclusively on documenting specific observable behaviors that lend . . . to quantifiable calculations of risk and strict timeframes" (p. 10). This is shift away from subjectively documenting families' experiences and understanding of child welfare involvement. Child welfare social workers find themselves assessing *what* parents have done to their children rather than *why* they have been abusive or neglectful (Davies & Collings, 2008). Additionally, studies have also suggested this more sterile approach to practice leaves child welfare social workers less satisfied with their careers due to higher levels of stress resulting from the need to meet specific and measurable outcomes.

There has been a push for child welfare to begin embracing the various theoretical perspectives developed in the social sciences to enhance work with children, youth, families, and, in particular, Black single mothers. By incorporating other perspectives, social workers are able to alter the oppressive condition of one group and change the oppressive nature of the system. Additionally, Black single mothers involved in the child welfare system need social workers who will "challenge the insidious cultural expectation of maternal perfection" (Davies & Collings, 2008, p. 14).

The following sections briefly introduce a number of theories that have been used in work with Black women and mothers. The discussion is not meant to be exhaustive, but rather to begin the process of exploration for the reader.

Africentric Theory

According to Swigonski (1996), Africentric theory addresses the importance of obtaining knowledge of multiple cultures from the perspective of those cultures. This new perspective can transform social work practice by allowing for enhanced self-awareness and the opportunity for deeper social worker–client relationships because the family is seen as the experts of their culture. This theory "reorganizes the frame of reference so that African culture, and worldview become the context of understanding Africans and African Americans" (p. 156). The foundation of the theory is in moving away from Eurocentric-based analysis of Black families in an effort to better understand the negative effects of racism and privilege on the Black family. Finally, Africentric theory takes a holistic stance, recognizing the interconnectedness of "all things and the oneness of mind, body, and spirit; development of collective rather than individual identity" (p. 157). Graham (1999) also includes "the spiritual nature of human beings, and the value of interpersonal relationships" (p. 112) to this list.

Antiracist/Antidiscriminatory Practice

Antiracism is a response to the wider societal and historical issues of slavery, colonialism, and capitalism. This idea has been conceptualized to ameliorate institutionalized racism by transforming the social relations between dominant and subordinate group members. Antiracist social work practice takes this theory a step further by not only addressing institutional oppression, but interpersonal oppression as well. Antiracist practice is new to the field of social work; therefore, there is little empirical knowledge with regard to its effectiveness. Keating (2000) notes, however, that there have been some promising contributions to the field of antidiscriminatory social work practice. This practice "has at its core meaning social work practice that is working against all forms of discrimination and oppression" by "understanding racism, oppression, and discrimination have created barriers to opportunities in the wider society and social worker awareness of personal biases, attitudes, and stereotypes" (Graham, 1999, p. 105).

Feminist Psychoanalytic Theory

To continue the conversation started by Davies and Collings (2008), "feminist psychoanalytic thinking provides a rich resource for child welfare practice" (p. 15). This theory takes into account the emotional reactions of families and develops ways to address those reactions. This theory is about understanding emotional triggers, addressing them, and supporting the family to address them. To carry this further, feminist psychoanalytic theory evaluates the psychological consequences of "oppression and how differences in race, culture, and class can have an impact on the therapeutic relationship" (Davies & Collings, 2008, p. 14). With this theory, not only is the child's development the focus of intervention, but the mother's needs and development within the social context in which women raise their children are also considered. Finally, when considering child welfare assessment, this theory suggests that social workers should consider "material and psychological deprivation" (Davies & Collings, 2008, p. 14).

Intersectional Theory

The concept of intersectionality was introduced in Chapter One. As a theory, intersectionality has been broadly and intensely studied since its inception in 1989. However, only recently has the theory been applied to social work practice. In their text, *Incorporating Intersectionality in Social Work Practice, Research, Policy and Education,* Murphy et al. (2009) present intersectional theory as a method to address "power imbalances of race, class, and gender" (p. 45) through social workers evaluating the ways in which power is expressed within their subconscious actions, comparing "their intentions, however altruistic, unintentional biases; and the objective outcomes of their interactions" (p. 46) with families. It is also key for social workers to understand the impact of families' past experiences of racism, sexism, classism on the their willingness to interact and receive services.

One way intersectional theory has shifted to practice is through McCall's typology of intersectional approaches. McCall (2005) provides a structural understanding of intersectional theory through three approaches—intercategorical, intracategorical, and anticategorical—that act as the foundation of intersectional research:

- *Intercategorical*: "race, class, and gender are understood to be an effect of structural inequalities, and individual identity is determined and shaped by the social structure" (p. 422).
- *Intracategorical*: "challenge the nature of essentialized, homogeneous social categorizations of gender, race, class . . . and simultaneously see the need for strategic essentializing of identities and communities to work toward particular political goals" (p. 423).
- *Anticategorical*: "challenge the idea of social categories as units of analysis and problematize the way in which categories are views as real, fixed, homogenous, and bound by social structure" (p. 423).

Intersectionality in Social Work Practice

"Critical reflection needs a powerful understanding of the relation between oppression and the intersection of gender, sexuality, class, and race" (Mattsson, 2014, p. 13). A reflection carried out without that kind of understanding risks reinforcing oppression and injustice.

How do we do this? In three easy steps.

1. Identify a critical incident and describe it with as much specific details as possible.
2. Make a critical reflection of your description by first identifying power relations within the incident.
3. Reconstruct and redevelop new and emancipating strategies for theory and practice as you identify and understand means of social change within the agency and your own scope of power.

Cultural Humility

To approach social work practice from a cultural humility framework is to advocate for "incorporating multicultural and intersectional understanding and analysis to improve practice" (Ortega & Faller, 2011, p. 32). This draws on the idea that these two concepts effectively represent the whole person, bringing attention to power differential in the helping relationship and "different past and present life experiences" (p. 32).

Cultural humility takes into account three dimensions of connectedness, similar to previously mentioned theories (Ortega & Faller, 2011):

1. *Self-awareness*: Who are you culturally?
2. *Characteristics of openness*: Do you accept that no one can know all there is to know about the world?
3. *Transcendence*: Can you see the world as more complex than you could ever imagine?

Critical Race Theory

Critical race theory speaks to addressing a broad social context of oppression while recognizing the intersection of multiple identities and then integrating social justice action (Caldwell, 2012). Further, critical race theory suggests cultural competence models fail to acknowledge the "socio-cultural mechanisms and institutional processes that prescribe and proscribe social injustices" (Ortega & Faller, 2011, p. 29).

This theory focuses on several core components (Caldwell, 2012):

- Social construction of race
- Pervasiveness of race and racism
- Microaggressions
- Eurocentrism of evidence-based practices
- Commitment to social justice
- Listening to marginalized voices to strengthen social work practice

Future Practice

When considering future practice, remember to think outside of the proverbial box. Working with Black single mothers means seeing beyond the allegations and understanding the systemic barriers they face. It means identifying ways to address oppression at all levels of social work practice—micro, mezzo, and macro. Child welfare social workers and professionals must pull from various knowledge bases and continually advocate on behalf of these families. Understanding the impact of combining historical and theoretical perspectives to develop future practice is ultimately what will lead to a transformation of the child welfare system.

Micro–Mezzo–Macro Practice

The field of social work encompasses three main levels of practice and intervention. *Micro practice* refers to the work social workers do on an interpersonal level with children, youth, and families. *Mezzo practice* seeks to address issues and concerns on a larger scale by focusing on the way community partners interact with families. *Macro practice* is about the foundation of social work; that is, social justice and implementing changes to policies. Social workers have the opportunity to support Black single mothers in processing their experiences of oppression and trauma, addressing community incidents of oppression, and effecting policy changes.

"Microlevel interventions focus on work with people individually, in families, or in small groups to foster changes within personal functioning, in social relationships, and in the ways people interact with social and institutional resources" (Miley, O'Melia, & DuBois, 2012, p. 9). Micro practice gives the social worker the opportunity to utilize generalist social work practice, which includes clinical interventions, crisis interventions, and family therapy. Typically, social workers with clinical licenses tend to feel most comfortable at the micro level because of their clinical education and training. This level provides the opportunity for the social worker to directly address the internalized and interpersonal oppression Black single mothers may be experiencing. Techniques such as cognitive-behavioral therapy, psychoeducation on oppression and how it manifests, processing, and trauma-informed clinical interventions help to alleviate the impact of oppression in the midst of the child welfare experience.

Mezzo practice focuses on change "within organizations and formal groups, including their structures, goals, and functions" (Miley et al., 2012, p. 9). This level of practice focuses on identifying ways in which the child welfare agency's community partners and referral agencies can best work with Black single mothers. Consider the earlier discussion on TANF sanctions; in order for Black single mothers to obtain day care vouchers so they are able to attend work and/or educational programs, some agencies require the mother to already be working. This poses an issue because taking a newborn or a child to a job interview will likely preclude the mother from obtaining employment. Through mezzo-level practice, social workers intervene by advocating on behalf of the mother while teaching her ways to advocate for herself. Mezzo practice does not include clinically specific interventions, but requires a level of critical thinking and practicing outside of what traditionally occurs within a child welfare agency.

At the mezzo level of social work practice, social workers "work to achieve social change through neighborhood organizing, community planning, locality development, public education, policy development and social action" (Miley et al., 2012, p.10). Child welfare social workers often find themselves working with multiple families who have multiple children, and this level of practice may seem impossible. However, promoting child abuse and neglect prevention campaigns, speaking out about oppression experienced by Black single mothers through testimony to policymakers, and supporting a mother to organize her community around experiences of oppression are all ways in which child welfare social workers can be involved at the macro level. Several child welfare agencies across the United States hire social workers to work specifically in developing policy specific to assessments, best practices, and quality improvement. Those social workers who have case responsibility can act as catalysts for change at the macro level by supporting Black single mothers to find and use their voice in enacting policy changes.

There is likely a level of practice at which each child welfare social worker is most comfortable working within or implementing in his or her practice. However, in child welfare, it is imperative for social workers to continually focus on each family from every level and perspective. This means tying together the four levels of oppression and the three levels of practice to develop a holistic approach to working with Black single mothers and their children, because the oppression they are experiencing is occurring at each intersection.

Racial Equity Strategy Areas (RESA)

In a document "meant to be a guide to those who are attempting to improve outcomes for children of color in the child welfare system" (Jackson, 2011, p. 15), the Black Administrators in Child Welfare (BACW) compiled strategies to address disproportionality. In "Reducing Disparities: 10 Racial Equity Strategy Areas (RESA) for Improving Outcomes for African American Children in Child Welfare," 10 RESA were outlined as improvements for child welfare. The third and fourth strategies focus on "engagement: parent and community and kinship services: effective and appropriate use," specifically addressing changes that can be made by the child welfare social workers at the micro level of practice.

RESA Standards

Engagement: Parent and Community

3.1 Acknowledge and embrace Black family child rearing practices that stress firmness, not abuse. Alternative child rearing practices should be recognized as healthy parenting.

3.2 Understand, acknowledge, and support the strength of the extended family.

3.3 Ensure and support non-traditional African American community support structures that can be used to fill service gaps and complement other services offered, such as churches and grassroots organizations.

3.4 Utilize culturally competent family assessment instruments and measures that speak to the nuances of African American family life, enhancing understanding of African American family needs.

3.5 Expand available resources for children and increase access to services through building community partners and relationships in the neighborhoods.

3.6 Address barriers to fully engaging parents and community participants in the development of resources and services for African American children.

Kinship Services: Effective and Appropriate Use

4.1 Realize that kinship care is preferred for African American children when their parents are unable to provide for them.

4.2 Understand, acknowledge, and support the strength of kinship families.

4.3 Ensure that the kinship triad (child, birth parent, and caregiver) is fully engaged in a collaborative relationship.
4.4 Ensure that kinship care services are family-centered, strengths-based and needs-driven with culturally appropriate assessment tools to document the services provided.
4.5 Willingness to be creative in the delivery of kinship care services.
4.6 Examine and modify policy procedures and licensing standards that create barriers for the placement of African American children in kinship placements.
4.7 Provide kinship families with flexible family support services that may or may not be solely supported by the child welfare system.

Transformational and Transactional Approaches

A key concept for child welfare social workers to understand is their role as team leaders. With the shift to strengths-based, solution-focused community partnering practice, social workers are expected to bring together multidisciplinary teams to work with families to support safety, permanence, and well-being. The profession of social work draws from various schools of thought to act as the foundation of practice; however, a key concept that has been missed in this drawdown is an understanding of leadership.

Roles of the Child Welfare Social Worker

Social workers have been given many titles/roles over the course of the profession. Child welfare social workers have multiple roles over the years that they are expected to succeed in to ensure that families are safe.

Review Table 4.2. Which roles are you, as a child welfare social worker or professional, most comfortable with? In which roles do you feel you need more guidance/mentoring?

One of the most important roles of the child welfare social worker is to act as a change agent. Being a change agent means leading others to and through the process of change. Acting as a change agent requires leadership skills. Two types of leadership are important to child welfare work: transactional leadership and transformation leadership. Transactional leadership focuses on a give-and-take relationship that is guided by appealing to self-interests and completing tasks in order to avoid punishment. This style of leadership is responsive and works best in crisis management and emergency situations. Through transactional leadership, the purpose and needs of case management are met, but it takes away from the skills, techniques, and spirit that is "social work."

Transactional leadership is defined by the elements of contingent reward and management by exception. Lai (2011) states "contingent reward, describes the extent to which effective transaction and exchange is set-up between leader and followers" (p. 3). Management by exception thus "describes whether leaders act to either prevent (active management) or resolve (passive management) problems as they arise" (p. 3). When child welfare social workers enter into this type of relationship with Black single mothers, the risk of meeting resistance, fear, and outright violence is increased.

Table 4.2 **Roles of the Child Welfare Social Worker**

Clinical Social Worker	Case Manager	Authority
Ally	Change Agent	Advocate
Team Coordinator	Team Leader	

In contrast, transformational leadership, first introduced by Burns in 1978, speaks to changing the culture of organizations to meet needs in a way that is interactive and inspiring. Burns (2010) defines transformational leadership as "a leadership style that is exemplified by charisma and shared vision between leaders and followers." This leadership style anticipates problems and emergencies by allowing social workers to think beyond what is organizationally expected, motiving them to move away from completing tasks to avoid punishment but rather completing them to get to the greatest good. Bernard Bass (1985) further expounded on Burns's theory through the dimensions of idealized influence, inspirational motivation, intellectual stimulation, and individual consideration.

Lai (2011) provides the following explanation for each:

> *Idealized influence,* also known as charismatic leadership, describes the extent to which leaders are capable of being role models to their followers and display solid moral and ethical principles.
>
> *Inspirational motivation* reflects the extent to which a leader is also capable of being a cheerleader, so to speak, on behalf of his or her followers.
>
> *Intellectual stimulation* instills creativity, and followers are encouraged to approach problems in new ways.
>
> *Individual consideration* reveals an investment in the development of their followers—they serve also as mentors and coaches, and take into account individual needs and desires within a group.

Because the current culture is to address presenting problems and practice crisis management, and because social workers are eager to return to the art of social work practice, child welfare social work requires a combination of these two theories of leadership. Transformational-transactional leadership theory provides for the opportunity for child welfare social workers to continue to work within the federal and local policies that govern child protection while transforming families by inspiring them to make changes not only in their own lives, but across the system. It is clear that those who are being marginalized by the system need those within the system to support their call to action. Child welfare social workers are the leaders of that change.

Teaching Self-Advocacy

Self-advocacy means to be able to speak on one's behalf to address negative outcomes and experiences of oppression. Black single mothers face myriad levels of oppression, as outlined throughout this text; however, all hope cannot be lost. It becomes the responsibility of the child welfare social worker to support the empowerment of these women to reach better outcomes not only for themselves, but also for their children. The empowerment perspective has been identified as a key set of assumptions, processes, and techniques to support women of color through their experience of oppression.

Membership in marginalized groups and the negative experiences that come along with these experiences strains Black single mothers' mental health and capacity to cope. Additionally, these experiences can leave women feeling a sense of powerlessness and hopelessness. Current models of social work focus on individual oppressions rather than understanding their intersectional nature and, therefore, more harmful experience of Black women. Instead of interventions focusing on supporting Black women to change their situation, focus on systemic change, and increase their actual power, the focus is on "assisting women to cope with or accept a difficult situation" (Gutierrez, 1990, p. 149).

An empowerment perspective assumes that issues of power and powerlessness are integral to the experience of women of color. "It proposes concrete and specific ways in which practice can help resolve the personal problems of women of color by increasing their power" (Gutierrez, 1990, p. 150).

Empowerment can be defined "as the process of is a process of increasing personal, interpersonal, or political power so that individuals can take action to improve their life situations" (Gutierrez, 1990, p. 151).

The process of empowerment occurs when Black single mothers obtain a sense of personal power that guides them to effecting change in all aspects of their lives—interpersonally, personally, and systemically. According to Gutierrez (1990), the literature suggests that four associated psychological changes are crucial for moving individuals from apathy and despair to action:

1 Increasing self-efficacy
2 Developing a group consciousness
3 Reducing self-blame
4 Accepting personal responsibility for change

It becomes part of the role of the social worker to support Black single mothers in this process. Within the helping relationship, child welfare social workers can use the following techniques presented by Gutierrez (1990) to move clients to a place of self-advocacy and empowerment:

Accepting the client's definition of the problem—this means going beyond the reason for agency involvement and understanding the crisis situation from the Black single mother's perspective.

Identifying and building upon existing strengths—this goes back to the strengths-based paradigm used across the country in child welfare practice. When a Black single mother is able to see the things she is doing well for her family, she is more likely to feel empowered and to be more involved in the process of change.

Engaging in a power analysis of the client's situation—the social worker partners with the Black single mother to help her ascertain the situations she has control over, the situations she will have control over in the future, and the situation she will need support in overcoming.

Teaching specific skills—this concept goes beyond teaching coping and parenting skills, but also means to teach or support the learning of vocational and tangible employment skills.

Mobilizing resources and advocating for clients—referring families to services with their specific needs in mind is key to empowerment. When social workers demonstrate a genuine interest in the needs and challenges of Black single mothers, there is a healthier helping relationship, and more opportunity to use that stronger relationship to effect change.

Clinical Supervision

Supervision is the time social workers have the opportunity to practice and hone their social work skills. It provides the opportunity for social workers to integrate policies, procedures, and social work practice. Supervision time should been as a "sacred space" that allows time and space for monitoring, evaluation, reflection, and refocusing. It is imperative that supervision is not solely seen from the perspective of ensuring that case management responsibilities are completed, but also as a means to support the clinical growth and knowledge of the social workers being supervised. Supervision is the time for the social worker to provide a clear and truthful account of what is happening with the families being supported, as well as to gain clinical insight on ways to enhance the client's resilience and build on their strengths.

Supervision has three goals: management, education, and support. The management piece focuses on the day-to-day processes of a unit, as well as ensuring that policies and practices are being followed. Education focuses on imparting knowledge about best practices and ensuring that this new knowledge is evident in practice. Finally, support is about providing the time and space for social workers to express their feelings and emotions regarding their cases and the work before them. This is a time to support social workers through the stresses they face and in whatever way alleviates this stress. Clinical supervision should enable social workers to regain the art of thinking creatively and critically, allowing space for "out of the box" interventions.

Within child welfare, supervision and management should incorporate aspects of transactional leadership as well as transformation leadership. Transactional leadership speaks to ensuring that specific outcomes are reached, and that the unit's monthly statistics meet agency benchmarks. Transformational leadership is about inspiring workers to want to get to a place of practicing the art of social work by encouraging continued learning and providing additional support.

As in building relationships with clients, supervision is also about building a relationship together and setting the boundaries of that relationship. There should be the opportunity to openly discuss the expectations as well as the limitations of the working relationship (Aymer & Okitikpi, 2008).

Conclusion

Transforming the child welfare system and child welfare social work is about returning to the roots of social work practice by recalling theories of the past, while also integrating new learning. As social workers consider new ways to practice, it is imperative to have a certain level of comfort when practicing. The NASW (2008) Code of Ethics calls for social workers to work within their competence. This expectation does not change within the social justice context. Therefore, social workers should continue their study of the various theories presented, seek out other theoretical perspectives outside of social work, be involved in change movements, and ultimately understand that for Black single mothers involved with the child welfare system oppression goes beyond race and class.

References

Austin, M. (Ed.). (2014). *Social justice and social work: Rediscovering a core value of the profession*. Los Angeles, CA: Sage.

Aymer, C., & Okitikpi, T. (2008). *The art of social work practice*. Dorset, UK: Russell House Publishing.

Bass, B. (1985). Leadership: Good, better, best. *Organizational Dynamics, 13*(3), 26–40.

Bishop, A. (2002). *Becoming an ally: Breaking the cycle of oppression in people*. New York, NY: Zed Books.

Burns, J. M. (2010). *Leadership.* New York, NY: Harper Perennial.

Caldwell, B. (2012). Addressing intersectionality in the lives of women in poverty: Incorporating core components of a social work program into legal education. *Journal of Gender, Social Policy, and the Law, 20*(4), 823–846.

Council on Social Work Education. (2015). *Educational policy and accreditation standards.* Washington, DC: NASW

Davies, L., & Collings, S. (2008). Emotional knowledge for child welfare practice: Rediscovering our roots. *Smith College Studies in Social Work, 78*(1), 7–27.

Gil, D. G. (2013). *Confronting injustice and oppression: Concepts and strategies for social workers.* New York, NY: Columbia University Press.

Goldenberg, I. (1978). *Oppression and social intervention.* Chicago, IL: Nelson-Hall.

Graham, M. (1999). The African-centered worldview: Toward a paradigm for social work. *Journal of Black Studies, 30*(1), 103–122.

Gutierrez, L. M. (1990). Working with women of color: An empowerment perspective. *Social Work,* March, 150–153.

Jackson, S. (2011). Reducing disparities: 10 racial equity strategy areas for improving outcomes for African American children in child welfare. The Black Administrators in Child Welfare: A Guide to Practice and Policy Development. Retrieved April 30, 2015, from http://www.blackadministrators.org/pdf/RESA.pdf

Keating, F. (2000). Anti-racist perspectives: What are the gains for social work? *Social Work Education, 19*(1), 77–87.

Lai, A. (2011). Transformational-transactional leadership theory. 2011 AHS Capstone Projects. Paper 17. Retrieved April 30, 2015, from http://digitalcommons.olin.eud/ahs_capstone_2011/17

Mattsson, T. (2014). Intersectionality as a useful tool: Antioppressive social work and critical reflection. *Journal of Women and Social Work, 29*(1), 8–17.

McCall, L. (2005). The complexity of intersectionality. *Signs: Journal of Women in Culture and Society, 30*(3), 1771–1800.

Miley, K., O'Melia, M., & DuBois, B. (2012). *Generalist Social Work Practice: An Empowering Approach.* (7th ed.). Boston, MA: Pearson.

Murphy, Y., Hunt, V., Zajicek, A., Norris, A., & Hamilton, L. (2009). *Incorporating intersectionality in social work practice, research, policy, and education.* Washington, DC: NASW Press.

National Association of Social Workers. (2008). *Code of ethics.* Washington, DC: NASW

Ortega, R., & Faller, K. (2011). Training child welfare workers from an intersectional cultural humility perspective: A paradigm shift. *Child Welfare, 90*(5), 27–49.

Pickering, T. (2011). What does "transformation" mean and how can we avoid "reform" mistakes of the past. Transforming Education for a Promising Future. Retrieved March 22, 2015, from http://www.tracepickering.com/picks-blog-systems-learning-education/what-does-transformation-mean-and-how-can-we-avoid-reform-mistakes-of-the-past

Sen, A. (2009). *The idea of justice.* Cambridge, MA: Harvard University Press.

Swigonski, M.E. (1996). Challenging privilege through Africentric social work practice. *Social Work, 41*(2), 153–161.

Vincent, N.J. (2012). Exploring the integration of social justice into social work research curricula. *Journal of Social Work Education, 48*(2), 205–222.

INDEX

Note: Page numbers in *italics* indicate tables.

For Product Safety Concerns and Information please contact our EU representative GPSR@taylorandfrancis.com
Taylor & Francis Verlag GmbH, Kaufingerstraße 24, 80331 München, Germany

www.ingramcontent.com/pod-product-compliance
Ingram Content Group UK Ltd.
Pitfield, Milton Keynes, MK11 3LW, UK
UKHW021436080625
459435UK00011B/278
9781138903005